MEL

THE BA(5
SONGBOOK

BY JERRY SILVERMAN

Applicable to guitar, other fretted instruments & harmonica

The songs in this book are written in the keys of C, G, D, A, E major and A, D, E minor. The arrangements have been written variously for harmonicas tuned to F, C, G, A and E. For harmonica-guitar duets, obviously both instruments will have to be in the same key. However, if you are playing solo harmonica (or can get the guitarist to transpose), any one harmonica can play all of the songs merely by following the numbers. Standard diatonic harmonica symbols are used:

1. A number under a note indicates the hole through which breath is to be blown or drawn.

2. An arrow up (↑) indicates blow.

3. An arrow down (↓) indicates draw.

4. The length of the arrow indicates the relative time value of the note.

5. A circle around a number, e.g. ⑧, indicates that the note is to be played a half-tone lower. This is done by "forcing" the note – blowing or drawing harder than when playing the natural note.

**Visit us on the Web at http://www.melbay.com —
E-mail us at email@melbay.com**

2

Contents

Folk Songs

Blues

Love Songs

Bluegrass

Children's Songs

Abdullah Bulbul Amir

A Harmonica

By William Percy French

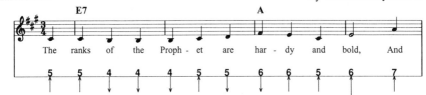

When they needed a man to encourage the van,
Or to harass the foe from the rear,
Storm fort or redoubt, they had only to shout
For Abdullah Bulbul Amir.

Now, the heroes were plenty and well known to fame,
Who fought in the ranks of the Czar,
But the bravest of these was a man by the name
Of Ivan Skavinsky Skivar.

He could imitate Pushkin, play poker and pool,
And strum on the Spanish guitar,
In fact, quite the cream of the Muscovite team
Was Ivan Skavinsky Skivar.

One day this bold Russian had shouldered his gun,
And donned his most truculent sneer,
Downtown he did go, where he trod on the toe
Of Abdullah Bulbul Amir.

"Young man," quoth Bulbul, "has your life grown so dull,
That you're anxious to end your career?
Vile infidel, know, you have trod on the toe
Of Abdullah Bulbul Amir."

Said Ivan, "My friend, your remarks in the end
Will avail you but little, I fear,
For you ne'er will survive to repeat them alive,
Mister Abdullah Bulbul Amir."

They fought all that night 'neath the yellow moonlight,
The din, it was heard from afar,
And huge multitudes came, so great was the fame
Of Abdul and Ivan Skivar.

As Abdul's long knife was extracting the life,
In fact he had shouted, "Huzzah!"
He felt himself struck by that wily Kalmuck,
Count Ivan Skavinsky Skivar.

There's a tomb made of gold where the Blue Danube rolls,
And 'graved there in characters clear,
Is, "Stranger, when passing, oh, pray for the soul
Of Abdullah Bulbul Amir."

A Muscovite maiden, her lone vigil keeps,
'Neath the light of the pale polar star,
And the name that she murmurs so oft as she weeps,
Is Ivan Skavinsky Skivar.

All My Trials

G Harmonica

If re-li-gion was a thing that mon-ey could buy, _____ The rich would live ____ and the poor would die. _____ All ____ my trials _ Lord, ____ soon ____ be o-ver, _____ Too late, my broth-ers, _ Too late, but nev-er mind, ____ All ____ my trials, Lord, ___ soon ____ be o-ver. ____

Chorus

I had a little book, 'twas given to me,
And every page spelled "Victory." *Chorus*

Hush, little baby, don't you cry,
You know your momma was born to die. *Chorus*

Amazing Grace

E Harmonica

Chorus

A-maz-ing _ grace, how sweet the sound, That _ saved a _ wretch like _ me, I ___ once was _ lost, but _ now I'm found, Was _ blind but _ now I see.

'Twas grace that taught my heart to fear,
And grace my fear relieved,
How precious did that grace appear,
The hour I first believed. *Chorus*

When we've been there ten thousand years,
Bright shining as the sun,
We've no less days to sing God's praise,
Than when we first begun. *Chorus*

Barb'ry Ellen

D Harmonica

In Scar-let-town where I was born, There was a fair maid dwell-in', Made

4 5 5 6   5 5 4 4   4 5 6 7 7   7 6 7

ev-'ry youth cry___ "Well a-day," Her name was Bar — b'ry El-len.

7 6 5   6 6   6 5 4   4 5 6 6   6 5 4

'Twas in the merry month of May,
When green buds, they were swellin',
Sweet William on his death-bed lay
For the love of Barb'ry Ellen.

He sent his servant to the town,
Where Barb'ry was a-dwellin',
"My master's sick and bids you come,
If you name be Barb'ry Ellen."

So slowly, slowly got she up,
And slowly she came nigh him,
And all she said when she got there,
"Young man, I think you're dyin'."

"Oh, yes, I'm sick, and very sick,
For death is in me dwellin'.
No better can I ever be,
If can't have Barb'ry Ellen."

Then lightly tripped she down the stairs,
He trembled like an aspen,
"'Tis vain, 'tis vain, my dear young man,
To pine for Barb'ry Ellen."

He turned his pale face to the wall,
For death was in him dwellin',
"Adieu, adieu, my friends all 'round,
Be kind to Barb'ry Ellen."

As she went down the long piney walk,
The birds, they kept a-singin',
They sang so clear, they seemed to say,
"Hard-hearted Barb'ry Ellen."

She looked to the east, she looked to the west,
She spied his corpse a-comin',
"Lay down, lay down that deathly frame
That I may look upon him."

"Farewell," she said, "ye virgins, all,"
And shun the fault I fell in,
Henceforth take warning by the fall
Of cruel Barb'ry Ellen."

They buried her in the old church yard
And he was buried nigh her,
On William's grave grew a red, red rose,
On Barb'ry's grew a brier.

They grew to the top of the old church wall,
Till they could grow no higher,
And there they tied a true lover's knot,
The red rose 'round the brier.

Cockles and Mussels
(Molly Malone)

C Harmonica

She was a fishmonger, but sure 'twas no wonder,
For so were her father and mother before,
And they pushed their wheelbarrow
 through streets broad and narrow,
Crying, "cockles and mussels alive, alive, o!" *Chorus*

She died of a "faver," and no one could save her,
And that was the end of sweet Molly Malone;
Her ghost wheels her barrow
 through streets broad and narrow,
Crying, "cockles and mussels alive, alive, o!" *Chorus*

The Cruel War

G Harmonica

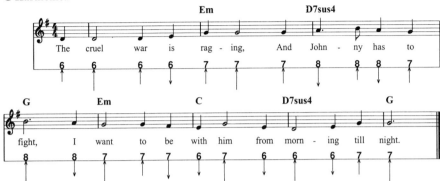

I'll go to your captain, get down upon my knees,
Ten thousand gold guineas I'll give for your release,

Ten thousand gold guineas, it grieves my heart so,
Won't you let me go with you? - Oh, no, my love, no.

Your captain calls for you, it grieves my heart so,
Won't you let me go with you? - Oh, no, my love, no.

Your waist is too slender, your fingers are too small,
Your cheeks are too rosy to face the cannonball.

Oh, Johnny, my Johnny, I think you are unkind,
I love you far better than all other mankind.

I'll pull back my hair, men's clothes I'll put on,
I'll pass for your comrade as we march along.

I'll pass for your comrade and none will ever guess,
Won't you let me go with you? - Oh, yes, my love, yes.

Delia

D Harmonica

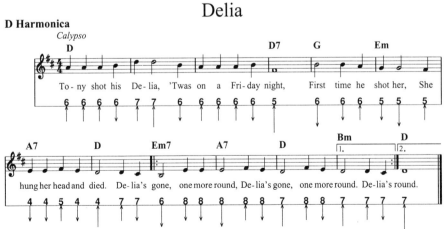

Send for the doctor - the doctor came too late,
Send for the minister to lay out Delia straight. *Chorus*

Delia, oh, Delia, where you been so long?
Everybody's talking about poor Delia's dead and gone. *Chorus*

Rubber-tired carriage - old-time broken hack,
Took poor Delia to the graveyard but didn't bring her back. *Chorus*

Drill, Ye Tarriers, Drill

C Harmonica

Our new foreman was Jim McCann,
By God, he was a blame mean man;
Last week a premature blast went off,
And a mile in the air went Big Jim Goff. *Chorus*

The next time pay day come around,
Jim Goff a dollar short was found,
When he asked what for come this reply,
"Yer docked fer the time you wuz up in the sky!" *Chorus*

Our boss was a fine man down to the ground,
And he married a lady six foot 'round,
She baked good bread and she baked it well,
But she baked it hard as the holes in hell. *Chorus*

Everybody Loves Saturday Night

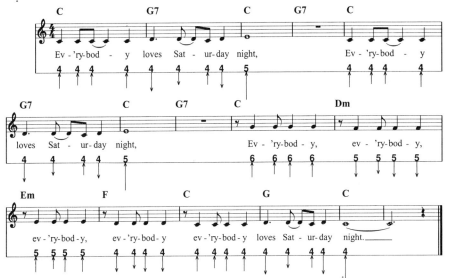

Nigerian:	Bobo waro fero Satodeh,	Russian:	Fsiem nravitsa subbota vietcher,
(original	Bobo waro fero Satodeh,		Fsiem nravitsa subbota vietcher,
language)	Bobo waro, bobo waro,		Fsiem nravitsa, fsiem nravitsa,
	Bobo waro, bobo waro,		Fsiem nravitsa, fsiem nravitsa,
	Bobo waro fero Satodeh.		Fsiem nravitsa subbota vietcher.

French:	Tout le monde aime Samedi soir,	Czech:	Kazhdi ma rad sabotu vietcher,
	Tout le monde aime Samedi soir,		Kazhdi ma rad sabotu vietcher,
	Tout le monde, tout le monde,		Kazhdi ma, kazhdi ma,
	Tout le monde, tout le monde,		Kazhdi ma, kazhdi ma,
	Tout le monde aime Samedi soir.		Kazhdi ma rad sabotu vietcher.

Yiddish:	Yeder eyner hot lieb Shabas ba nacht,	Spanish:	A todos le gusta la noche del Sabado,
	Yeder eyner hot lieb Shabas ba nacht,		A todos le gusta la noche del Sabado,
	Yeder eyner, yeder eyner,		A todos le gusta, a todos le gusta,
	Yeder eyner, yeder eyner,		A todos le gusta, a todos le gusta,
	Yeder eyner hot lieb Shabas ba nacht.		A todos le gusta la noche del Sabado.

Chinese:	Ren ren si huan li pai lu,	Ertruscan:	All the cats dig Saturday night the most,
	Ren ren si huan li pai lu.		All the cats dig Saturday night the most,
	Ren ren si, ren ren si,		All the cats, all the cats,
	Ren ren si, ren ren si,		All the cats, all the cats,
	Ren ren si huan li pai lu.		All the cats dig Saturday night the most.

The Gal I Left Behind Me

C Harmonica

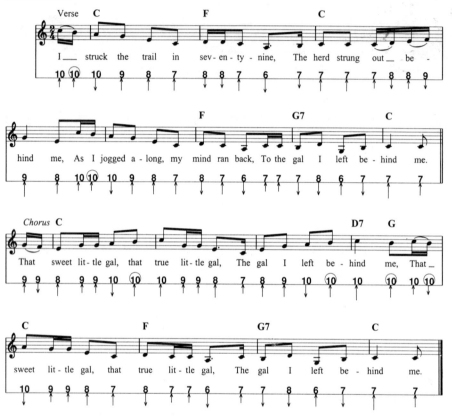

The wind did blow, the rain did fall,
The hail did fall and blind me,
I thought of the gal, that sweet little gal,
The gal I left behind me. *Chorus*

If ever I get off the trail
And the Indians they don't find me,
I'll make my way straight back again
To the gal I left behind me. *Chorus*

When we sold out I took the train,
I knew where I would find her,
When I got back we had a smack,
And that was no golderned liar. *Chorus*

Guantanamera

By José Martí
English lyrics by Jerry Silverman
Cuba

E Harmonica

Mi verso es de un verde claro,
Y de un carmin encendido.
Mi verso es de un verde claro,
Y de un carmin encendido.
Mi verso es un cierro herido,
Que busca en el monte amparo. *Chorus*

Con los pobres de la tierra,
Quiero yo mi suerte echar.
Con los pobres de la tierra,
Quiero yo mi suerte echar.
El arroyo de la sierra
Me complace mas que el mar. *Chorus*

My verse is a bright green color,
And also shades of bright carmine.
My verse is a bright green color,
And also shades of bright carmine.
A wounded fawn is my poem,
Seeking for peace on the mountain. *Chorus*

And all the poor of this planet,
My fate I'd gladly share with them.
And all the poor of this planet,
My fate I'd gladly share with them.
The rushing stream of the mountain
Means more to me than the ocean. *Chorus*

John B.

E Harmonica

Chorus: So hoist up the John B. sails,
See how the mainsail sets,
Send for the captain ashore, let me go home.
Let me go home, let me go home,
I feel so break up, I want to go home.

The first mate, oh, he got drunk,
Broke up the people's trunk,
Constable had to come and take him away,
Sheriff Johnstone please leave me alone,
I feel so break-up, I want to go home. *Chorus*

The poor cook, oh, he got fits,
Ate up all of the grits,
Then he took and threw away all of the corn.
Sheriff Johnstone please leave me alone,
This is the worst trip I ever been on. *Chorus*

John Henry

D Harmonica

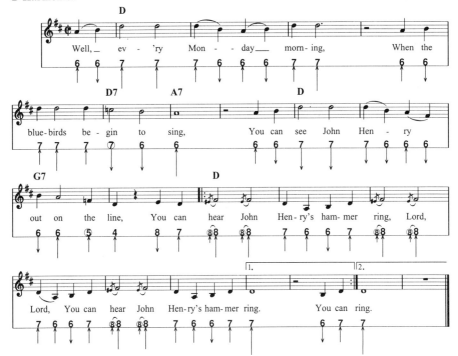

Well, ev-'ry Mon-day morn-ing, When the blue-birds be-gin to sing, You can see John Hen-ry out on the line, You can hear John Hen-ry's ham-mer ring, Lord, Lord, You can hear John Hen-ry's ham-mer ring. You can ring.

When John Henry was a little baby,
A-sitting on his papa's knee,
He picked up a hammer and a little piece of steel,
Said, "Hammer's gonna be the death of me," Lord, Lord,
"Hammer's gonna be the death of me."

Well, the captain said to John Henry,
"Gonna bring me a steam drill 'round,
Gonna bring me a steam drill out on the job,
Gonna whup that steel on down," Lord, Lord.
"Gonna whup that steel on down."

John Henry said to his captain,
"A man ain't nothin' but a man,
And before I let that steam drill beat me down,
I'll die with a hammer in my hand," Lord, Lord.
"I'll die with a hammer in my hand."

John Henry said to his shaker,
"Shaker, why don't you sing?
I'm a-throwin' twelve pounds from my hips on down,
Just listen to the cold steel ring," Lord, Lord.
"Listen to that cold steel ring."

John Henry said to his shaker,
"Shaker, why don't you pray?
'Cause if I miss this little piece of steel,
Tomorrow be your buryin' day," Lord, Lord.
"Tomorrow be your buryin' day."

John Henry was driving on the mountain,
And his hammer was flashing fire,
And the last words I heard that poor boy say,
"Gimme a cool drink of water 'fore I die," Lord, Lord.
"Gimme a cool drink of water 'fore I die,"

John Henry, he drove fifteen feet,
The steam drill only made nine,
But he hammered so hard that he broke his poor heart,
And he laid down his hammer and he died, Lord, Lord.
Laid down his hammer and he died.

They took John Henry to the graveyard
And they buried him in the sand,
And every locomotive comes a-roaring by says,
"There lies a steel-driving man," Lord, Lord.
"There lies a steel-driving man."

Johnny, I Hardly Knew You

C Harmonica

Chorus: With your drums and guns and guns and drums,
Hurroo! Hurroo!
With your drums and guns and guns and drums,
Hurroo! Hurroo!
With your drums and guns and guns and drums
The enemy nearly slew ye,
Oh, darling dear, ye look so queer,
Faith, Johnny, I hardly knew ye!

Where are your eyes that looked so mild,
Hurroo! Hurroo!
Where are your eyes that looked so mild,
Hurroo! Hurroo!
Where are your eyes that looked so mild
When my heart you so beguiled,
Why did you run from me and the child?
Why Johnny, I hardly knew ye! *Chorus*

Where are the legs with which you run,
Hurroo! Hurroo!
Where are the legs with which you run,
Hurroo! Hurroo!
Where are the legs with which you run,
When you went for to carry a gun?
Indeed, your dancing days are done,
Faith, Johnny, I hardly knew ye! *Chorus*

I'm happy for to see you home,
Hurroo! Hurroo!
I'm happy for to see you home,
Hurroo! Hurroo!
I'm happy for to see you home,
All from the Island of Ceylon,
So low in flesh so high in bone,
Faith, Johnny, I hardly knew ye! *Chorus*

Lord Randall

E Harmonica

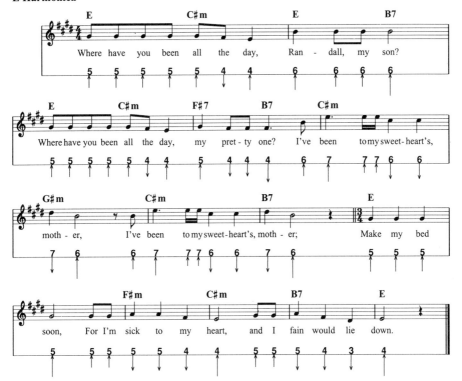

What have you been eating there, Randall, my son?
What have you been eating there, my pretty one?
Eels and eelbroth, Mother,
Eels and eelbroth, Mother. *Chorus*

Where did she get them from, Randall, my son?
Where did she get them from, my pretty one?
From hedges and ditches, Mother,
From hedges and ditches, Mother. *Chorus*

What was the color of their skin, Randall, my son?
What was the color of their skin, my pretty one?
Spickle and sparkle, Mother,
Spickle and sparkle, Mother. *Chorus*

What will you leave your brother, Randall, my son?
What will you leave your brother, my pretty one?
My gold and silver, Mother,
My gold and silver, Mother. *Chorus*

What will you leave your sweetheart, Randall, my son?
What will you leave your sweetheart, my pretty one?
A rope to hang her, Mother,
A rope to hang her, Mother. *Chorus*

The Midnight Special

G Harmonica

If you ever go to Houston, you'd better walk right,
And you better not stagger, and you better not fight,
'Cause the sheriff will arrest you and he'll carry you down,
And you can bet your bottom dollar you're Sugarland bound.
Chorus

Yonder comes Miss Rosie, tell me how do you know?
I know her by her apron and the dress she wore,
Umbrella on her shoulder, piece of paper in her hand,
Well, I heard her tell the captain, "I want my man." *Chorus*

Lord, Thelma said she loved me, but I believe she told a lie,
'Cause she hasn't been to see me since last July,
She brought me little coffee, she brought me little tea,
She brought me nearly everything but the jail house key.
Chorus

Well, the biscuits on the table, just as hard as any rock,
If you try to eat them, break a convict's heart,
My sister wrote a letter, my mother wrote a card,
"If you want to come to see us, you'll have to ride the rods."
Chorus

I'm goin' away to leave you, and my time it ain't long,
The man is gonna call me, and I'm goin' home,
Then I'll be done all my grievin', whoopin', hollerin' and a-cryin';
Then I'll be done all my studyin' 'bout my great long time. *Chorus*

Nine Hundred Miles

C Harmonica

Well, the train I ride on is a hundred coaches long,
You can hear the whistle blow a hundred miles.
And the lonesome whistle call is the mournfullest of all,
'Cause it's nine hundred miles from my home. *Chorus*

Well, I'll pawn you my watch and I'll pawn you my chain,
Pawn you my gold diamond ring.
If that train runs me right I'll be home Saturday night,
'Cause I'm nine hundred miles from my home. *Chorus*

If my woman says so, I'll railroad no more,
But I'll sidetrack that wheeler and go home.
If that train runs me right I'll be home Saturday night,
'Cause it's nine hundred miles from my home. *Chorus*

The Ox-Driving Song

C Harmonica

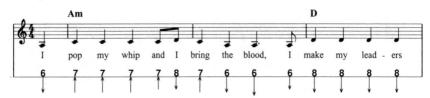

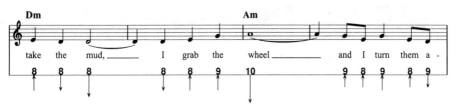

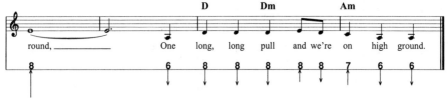

Chorus: To my roll, to my roll, to my ride-e-o,
To my roll, to my roll, to my ride-e-o,
To my ride-e-o, to my ru-de-o,
To my roll, to my roll, to my ride-e-o.

On the fourteenth day of October-o,
I hitched my team in order-o,
To drive to the hills of Saludio,
To my roll, to my roll, to my ride-e-o. *Chorus*

When I got there the hills were steep,
A tender-hearted person'd weep
To hear me cuss and pop my whip,
To see my oxen pull and slip. *Chorus*

When I get home I'll have revenge,
I'll land my family among my friends,
I'll bid adieu to the whip and line,
And drive no more in the wintertime. *Chorus*

Shenandoah

D Harmonica

Oh, Shen-an-doah, I long to hear you, A - way, you roll-ing riv-er Oh,

Shen-an-doah, I long to hear you, A - way, we're bound a-way, 'Cross the wide Mis - sour - i

The white man loved the Indian maiden,
Away, you rolling river,
With notions his canoe was laden, *Chorus*

Oh, Shenandoah, I love your daughter,
Away, you rolling river,
I'll take her 'cross the rolling water, *Chorus*

Oh, Shenandoah, I'm bound to leave you,
Away, you rolling river,
Oh, Shenandoah, I'll not deceive you, *Chorus*

Sometimes I Feel Like a Motherless Child

G Harmonica

Some-times I feel like a moth - er - less child, Some-times I feel like a

moth - er - less child, Some-times I feel like a moth - er - less child, A

long way from home, A long way from home, True be -

liev - er A long way from home, A long way from home.

Sometimes I feel like I'm almost gone,
Sometimes I feel like I'm almost gone,
Sometimes I feel like I'm almost gone,
Way up in that heavenly land.

Way up in that heavenly land,
True believer!
Way up in that heavenly land,
Way up in that heavenly land.

20

The Streets of Laredo

D Harmonica

"I see by your outfit that you are a cowboy,"
These words he did say as I boldly walked by.
"Come sit down beside me and hear my sad story,
I'm shot in the breast and I know I must die.

"It was once in the saddle I used to go dashing,
Once in the saddle I used to go gay;
First down to Rosie's and then to the card-house,
Got shot in the breast and I'm dying today."

"Get sixteen gamblers to carry my coffin,
Let six jolly cowboys come sing me a song,
Take me to the graveyard and lay the sod o'er me,
For I'm a young cowboy and I know I've done wrong."

"Oh, beat the drum slowly and play the fife lowly,
Play the dead march as you carry me along.
Put bunches of roses all over my coffin,
Roses to deaden the clods as they fall."

Sweet Betsy from Pike

C Harmonica

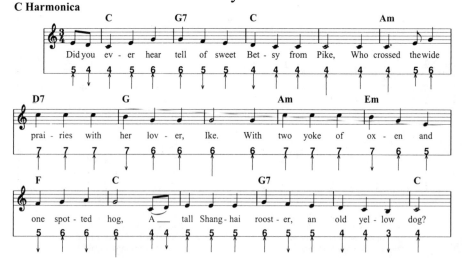

One evening quite early they camped on the Platte,
'Twas near by the road on a green shady flat;
Where Betsy, quite tired, lay down to repose,
While with wonder Ike gazed on his Pike County rose.
Chorus

Out on the prairie one bright starry night
They broke out the whisky and Betsy got tight.
She sang and she shouted and danced o'er the plain,
And showed her bare arse to the whole wagon train.
Chorus

The Injuns came down in a wild yelling horde,
And Betsy was skeered they would scalp her adored.
Behind the front wagon wheel Betsy did crawl,
And fought off the Injuns with musket and ball. *Chorus*

They stopped at Salt Lake to inquire the way,
Where Brigham declared that sweet Betsy should stay,
But Betsy got frightened and ran like a deer,
While Brigham stood pawing the ground like a steer.
Chorus

The Shanghai ran off and their cattle all died,
That morning the last piece of bacon was fried,
Poor Ike got discouraged and Betsy got mad,
The dog drooped his tail and looked wondrously sad.
Chorus

They soon reached the desert where Betsy gave out,
And down in the sand she lay rolling about,
While Ike in great terror looked on in surprise,
Saying, "Betsy, get up, you'll get sand in your eyes."
Chorus

The alkali desert was burning and bare,
And Isaac's soul shrank from the death that lurked there,
"Dear old Pike County, I'll go back to you,"
Says Besty, "You'll go by yourself if you do." *Chorus*

They swam the wide rivers and crossed the tall peaks,
They camped on the prairie for weeks upon weeks,
Starvation and cholera, hard work and slaughter,
They reached California spite of hell and high water. *Chorus*

One morning they climbed up a very high hill,
And with wonder looked down upon old Placerville,
Ike shouted and said, as he cast his eyes down,
"Sweet Betsy, my darling, we've got to Hangtown." *Chorus*

Lone Ike and Sweet Betsy attended a dance,
And Ike wore a pair of his Pike County pants,
Sweet Betsy was dressed up in ribbons and rings,
Says Ike, "You're an angel, but where are your wings?" *Chorus*

A miner said, "Betsy, will you dance with me?"
"I will, you old hoss, if you don't make too free,
But don't dance me hard-do you want to know why?
Doggone ye, I'm chock-full of strong alkali!" *Chorus*

Long Ike and Sweet Betsy got married, of course,
But Ike, getting jealous, obtained a divorce,
And Betsy, well satisfied, said with a shout,
"Goodbye, you big lummox, I'm glad you backed out!" *Chorus*

Take This Hammer

E Harmonica

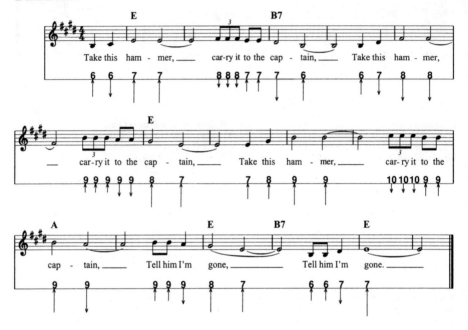

If he asks you, was I laughin',
If he asks you, was I laughin',
If he asks you, was I laughin',
Tell him I was cryin', tell him I was cryin'.

If he asks you, was I runnin',
If he asks you, was I runnin',
If he asks you, was I runnin',
Tell him I was flyin', tell him I was flyin'.

I don't want no cornbread and molasses,
I don't want no cornbread and molasses,
I don't want no cornbread and molasses,
They hurt my pride, they hurt my pride.

I don't want no cold iron shackles,
I don't want no cold iron shackles,
I don't want no cold iron shackles,
Around my leg, around my leg.

Repeat first verse

Waltzing Matilda

C Harmonica

Australia

Down came a jumbuck to drink at the waterhole,
Up jumped the swagman and grabbed him with glee;
And he sang as he stowed him away in his tuckerbag,
"You'll come a-waltzing Matilda with me." *Chorus*

Down came the squatter a-riding his thoroughbred;
Down came the policeman-one, two, three;
"Whose is the jumbuck you've got in your tuckerbag?
You'll come a-waltzing Matilda with me." *Chorus*

But the swagman he got up and he jumped into the waterhole,
Drowning himself by the coolibar tree;
And his ghost may be heard as it sings in the billabong,
"Who'll come a-waltzing Matilda with me." *Chorus*

Wheel of Fortune

C Harmonica

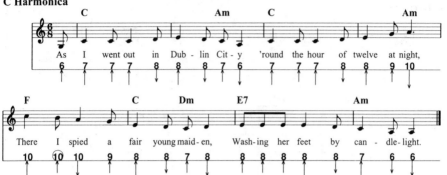

As I went out in Dub - lin Cit - y 'round the hour of twelve at night,
6 7 7 7 8 8 8 7 6 7 7 7 8 8 9 10

There I spied a fair young maid- en, Wash-ing her feet by can - dle- light.
10 10 10 9 8 8 7 8 8 8 8 8 8 7 6 6

Chorus: She had twenty, eighteen, sixteen, fourteen,
Twelve, ten, eight, six, four, two, none.
She had nineteen, seventeen, fifteen, thirteen,
Eleven, nine, seven, five, three and one.

First she washed them, then she dried them,
'Round her shoulder wore a towel,
And in all my life I ne'er did see
Such a fine young girl, upon my soul. *Chorus*

'Round and 'round the wheel of fortune,
Where she stops it wearies me,
Fair young girls are all deceiving,
Sad experience teaches me. *Chorus*

When the Saints Go Marching In

E Harmonica

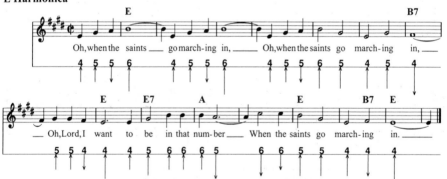

Oh, when the saints __ go march-ing in, ____ Oh, when the saints go march-ing in, __
4 5 5 6 4 5 5 6 4 5 5 6 5 4 5 4

__ Oh, Lord, I want to be in that num- ber __ When the saints go march-ing in. ____
5 5 4 4 4 5 6 6 6 5 6 6 5 5 4 4 4

And when the sun refuse to shine,
And when the sun refuse to shine,
Oh, Lord, I want to be in that number,
When the sun refuse to shine.

And when the moon drips red with blood,
And when the moon drips red with blood,
Oh, Lord, I want to be in that number,
When the moon drips red with blood.

And when the Revelation comes,
And when the Revelation comes,
Oh, Lord, I want to be in that number,
When the Revelation comes.

Repeat first verse

Willie the Weeper

G Harmonica

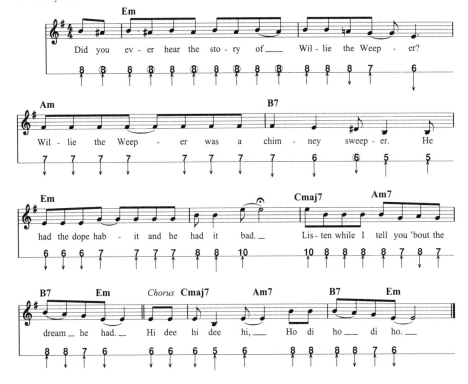

He went down to the dope house one Saturday night,
When he knew that all the lights would be burning bright.
He must have smoked a dozen pills or more,
When he woke up he was on a foreign shore. *Chorus*

Well, the Queen of Sheba was the first he met,
She called him her darling and her loving pet.
She gave him a great big automobile,
With a diamond headlight and a gold steering wheel. *Chorus*

He landed with a splash in the River Nile,
A-riding a domesticated crocodile.
He winked at Cleopatra - she said, "Ain't he a sight?
How about a date for next Saturday night?" *Chorus*

Down in Monte Carlo he won every bet,
Made a million dollars just a-playing roulette.
He broke the Czar of Russia-what a joke!
So Willie took another pill and rolled a smoke. *Chorus*

He had a million cattle and he had a million sheep,
He had a million vessels the ocean deep.
He had a million dollars in nickels and dimes,
He knew 'cause he had counted it a million times.
Chorus

He landed in New York one evening late,
And asked his sugar for an after date,
Willie got funny, she began to shout -
When, bim bam boo! The dope gave out. *Chorus*

The Wraggle-taggle Gypsies

C Harmonica

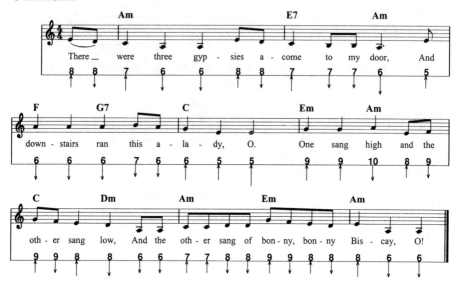

Then she pulled off her silk finished gown,
And put on hose of leather-o.
The ragged, ragged rags about our door,
And she's gone with the wraggle-taggle gypsies-o!

It was late last night when my lord came home,
Inquiring for his a-lady-o.
The servants said on every hand:
She's gone with the wraggle-taggle gypsies-o.

O, saddle to me my milk-white steed,
And go fetch me my pony-o!
That I may ride and seek my bride,
Who is gone with the wraggle-taggle gypsies-o.

O, he rode high and he rode low,
He rode through wood and copses-o,
Until he came to a wide open field,
And there he espied his a-lady o.

What makes you leave your house and land?
What makes you leave your money-o?
What makes you leave your new-wedded lord
To go with the wraggle-taggle gypsies-o?

What care I for my house and land?
What care I for my money-o?
What care I for my new-wedded lord?
I'm off with the wraggle-taggle gypsies-o!

Last night you slept on a goose-feather bed,
With the sheet turned down so bravely-o!
Tonight you'll sleep in a cold, open field,
Along with the wraggle-taggle gypsies-o!

What care I for a goose-feather bed,
With the sheet turned down so bravely-o!
For tonight I shall sleep in a cold, open field,
Along with the wraggle-taggle gypsies-o!

Abilene

E Harmonica

Ab - i - lene, — Ab - i - lene, — Pret - ti - est town I

ev - er seen, — Folks out there — don't treat you mean, — In Ab - i -

lene, my Ab - i - lene. _____

Sit alone every night,
Watch the trains roll out of sight,
Don't I wish they were carrying me
To Abilene, my Abilene.

Crowded city, ain't nothin' free;
Ain't nothin' in this crowd for me.
Wish to my God that I could be
In Abilene, my Abilene.

Alabama Bound

F Harmonica

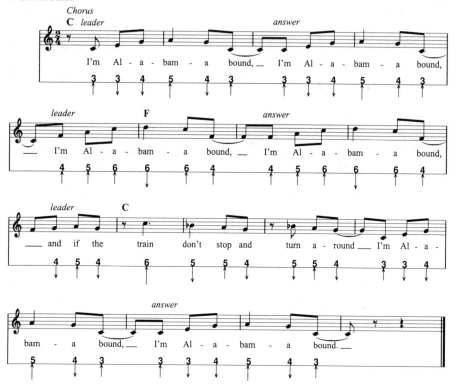

Oh, don't you leave me here, Oh, don't you leave me here,
Oh, don't you leave me here, Oh, don't you leave me here,
But if you must go anyhow,
Leave me a dime for beer, Leave me a dime for beer.

Oh, well the preacher preached, Oh, well the preacher
preached,
And pass the hat around, And pass the hat around,
Crying, "Brothers and sisters, all,
Just leave your cash with me."

Oh, don't you be like me, Oh, don't you be like me,
Oh, don't you be like me, Oh, don't you be like me,
Drink your good old cherry wine
And let that whisky be, And let that whisky be.

Oh, well your hair don't curl, Oh, well your hair don't
curl,
And your eyes ain't blue, And your eyes ain't blue,
Well if you don't want me, sweet Polly Ann,
Oh, well I don't want you, Oh, well I don't want you.

Repeat first verse

Another Man Done Gone

C Harmonica

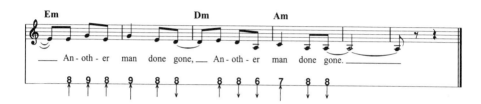

I didn't know his name,
I didn't know his name,
I didn't know his name,
Another man done gone.

He had a long chain on,
He had a long chain on,
He had a long chain on,
Another man done gone.

He killed another man,
He killed another man,
He killed another man,
Another man done gone.

I don't know where he's gone,
I don't know where he's gone,
I don't know where he's gone,
Another man done gone.

Repeat first verse

Backwater Blues

F Harmonica

Well, it thundered and it lightninged and the winds began to blow,
Well, it thundered and it lightninged and the winds began to blow,
There was thousands of people didn't have no place to go.

I woke up this morning, couldn't even get out my door,
I woke up this morning, couldn't even get out my door,
Enough trouble to make a poor boy wonder where he gonna go.

I went out to the lonesome, high old lonesome hill,
I went out to the lonesome, high old lonesome hill,
And looked down on the old house where I used to live.

Backwater blues have caused me to pack up my things and go,
Backwater blues have caused me to pack up my things and go,
'Cause my house fell down and I can't live there no more.

Been In the Pen so Long

E Harmonica

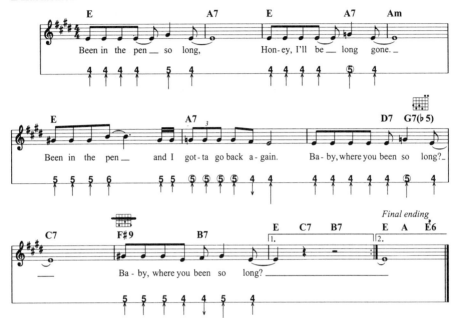

Awful lonesome, all alone and blue,
Awful lonesome, all alone and blue,
All alone and blue, no one to tell my troubles to,
Baby, where you been so long?
Baby, where you been so long?

Some folks crave for Memphis, Tennessee,
Some folks crave for Memphis, Tennessee,
Some folks crave for Memphis, Tennessee,
But New Orleans is good enough for me,
New Orleans is good enough for me.

Repeat first verse

Betty and Dupree

A Harmonica

Bet-ty __ told Du-pree, __ "I want a dia-mond ring."__

5 5   5 5 4   6 6 6 6   ⑤ 4 4

Bet-ty __ told _ Du-pree, _____ "I want a dia-mond ring."__ Du-pree __ told

6 6   6 6 5 5   7 7 7 6 6   5 5   5 4

Bet-ty, __ "I'll give you most an-y - thing."__ He said,

5 4   6 6 6 6 ⑤ 4   4   5 5

He said, "Lie down, little Betty, see what tomorrow brings,"
He said, "Lie down, little Betty, see what tomorrow brings,"
It may bring you sunshine, may bring you that diamond ring."

Then he got his pistol, went to the jewelry store,
He got his pistol, went to the jewelry store.
He killed a policeman and he wounded four or five more.

Then he went to the post office to get his evening mail,
Went to the post office to get his evening mail,
Sheriff caught poor Dupree and put him in that old Atlanta jail.

Dupree's mother said to Betty, "Looka here what you done done,"
She said to Betty, "See what you done done.
Made my boy rob and steal and now he's gonna be hung."

"Give my daddy my clothes - poor Betty, give her my shoes,
Give my daddy my clothes, give my baby, Betty, my shoes.
If anybody asks you, say I died with the heartbreaking blues."

Sail on, sail on, sail on, Dupree, sail on.
Sail on, sail on, sail on, Dupree, sail on.
You don't mind sailing, you'll be gone so doggone long.

The Blues Ain't Nothin'

D Harmonica

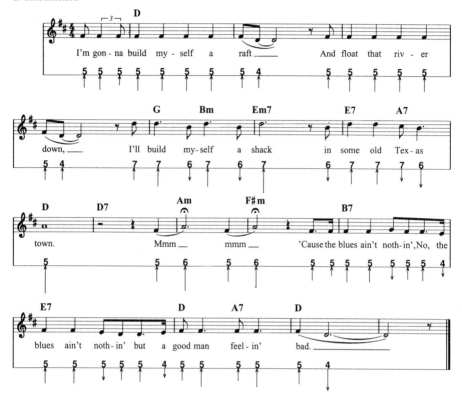

I'm goin' down on the levee,
Goin' to take myself a rockin' chair,
If my lovin' gal don't come,
I'll rock away from there.
Mmm - mmm. . .
'Cause the blues ain't nothin',
No, the blues ain't nothin'
But a good man feelin' bad.

Why did you leave me blue?
Why did you leave me blue?
All I can do is sit
And cry and cry for you.
Mmm - mmm. . .
'Cause the blues ain't nothin',
No, the blues ain't nothin'
But a good man feelin' bad.

Chilly Winds

C Harmonica

I'm going where there ain't no ice and snow, darlin' baby,
I'm going where there ain't no ice and snow,
When I'm gone to my long lonesome home.

I'm going where the folks all know my name, darlin' baby,
I'm going where the folks all know my name,
When I'm gone to my long lonesome home.

I'm here in the jailhouse on my knees, darlin' baby,
I'm here in the jailhouse on my knees,
When I'm gone to my long lonesome home.

Make me a pallet on your floor, darlin' baby,
Make me a pallet on your floor,
When I'm gone to my long lonesome home.

Now, who'll be your daddy when I'm gone, darlin' baby,
Who'll be your daddy when I'm gone,
When I'm gone to my long lonesome home?

Repeat first verse

Darlin'

G Harmonica

If I'd a-known my captain was blind, darlin', darlin', If I'd a-known my captain was blind, darlin', darlin', If I'd a-known my captain was blind, I wouldn't have gone to work till half past nine. Darlin', darlin'.

Asked my captain for the time of day, darlin', darlin',
Asked my captain for the time of day, darlin', darlin',
Asked my captain for the time of day,
He got so mad he threw his watch away - darlin', darlin'.

Fight my captain and I'll land in jail, darlin', darlin',
Fight my captain and I'll land in jail, darlin', darlin',
Fight my captain and I'll land in jail,
Nobody 'round to go my bail - darlin', darlin'.

If I'd a-had my weight in lime,* darlin', darlin',
If I'd a-had my weight in lime, darlin', darlin',
If I'd a-had my weight in lime,
I'd have whipped that captain till he went stone blind-darlin', darlin'.

If I'd a-listened to what my mama said, darlin', darlin',
If I'd a-listened to what my mama said, darlin', darlin',
If I'd a-listened to what my mama said,
I'd be at home and in my mama's bed-darlin', darlin'.

Repeat First Verse

* i.e. If I were a white man on even terms for a fair fight.

Deep-River Blues

E Harmonica

Let it rain, __ Let it pour, __ Let it rain __ a whole lot more, __ Since
Let the rain __ drive right on, __ Let the waves __ sweep a - long, __ 'Cause

I've got them deep riv-er blues. __   deep riv-er blues. __
I've got them

My old gal's gone away,
Said she'd be back some old day,
Now, I've got them deep-river blues.
There ain't no one to cry for me,
I'm all alone now, don't you see,
And I've got them deep-river blues.

If my boat sinks with me,
I'll go down, don't you see,
'Cause I've got them deep-river blues.
Now I'm goin' to say goodbye,
And if I sink just let me die,
'Cause I've got them deep-river blues.

Give me back my old boat,
I'm gonna sail, if she'll float,
'Cause I've got them deep-river blues.
I'm goin' back to Mussel Shoals,
Times are better there, I'm told,
'Cause I've got them deep-river blues.

East Colorado Blues

F Harmonica

Each verse is sung twice, as in the music.

This is the hammer that killed John Henry,
But it won't kill me,
No, it won't kill me,
No, it won't kill me,

Well, John Henry, he left his hammer,
Lyin' side the road,
Lyin' side the road,
Lyin' side the road,

This old hammer fallin' from my shoulder,
The steel goin' down,
The steel goin' down,
The steel goin' down,

When you hear my hammer ringin',
Steel runnin' like lead,
Steel runnin' like lead,
Steel runnin' like lead,

Take this hammer, carry it to the captain,
Tell him I'm gone,
Yes, tell him I'm gone,
Lawd, tell him I'm gone.

Easy Rider

A Harmonica

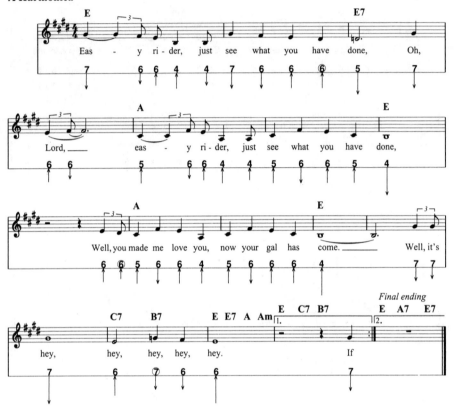

If I was a catfish, swimmin' in the deep blue sea, Oh Lord,
If I was a catfish, swimmin' in the deep blue sea,
I would swim across the ocean, bring my baby back to me,
Well, it's hey, hey, hey, hey, hey.

I'm goin' away, rider, and I won't be back till fall, Oh Lord.
I'm goin' away, rider, and I won't be back till fall,
And if I find me a good man, I won't be back at all.
Well, it's hey hey, hey, hey, hey.

Hesitation Blues

C Harmonica

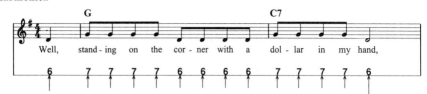

Well, the eagle on the dollar says, "In God we trust,"
Woman wants a man, she wants to see a dollar first. *Chrous*

Well, you hesitate by one, and you hesitate by two,
Angels up in heaven singing hesitatin' blues. *Chorus*

House of the Rising Sun

C Harmonica

If I had listened to what mama said,
I'd 'a' been at home today,
Being so young and foolish, poor girl,
Let a gambler lead me astray.

My mother, she's a tailor,
She sells those new blue jeans,
My sweetheart, he's a drunkard, Lord,
Drinks down in New Orleans.

The only thing a drunkard needs
Is a suitcase and a trunk,
The only time he's satisfied
Is when he's on a drunk.

One foot is on the platform,
And the other one on the train,
I'm going back to New Orleans
To wear that ball and chain.

Go tell my baby sister,
Never do like I have done,
To shun that house in New Orleans,
They call the Rising Sun.

I'm going back to New Orleans,
My race is almost run,
Going back to end my life
Beneath the Rising Sun.

I Know You, Rider

F Harmonica

I know you, rid - er, _____ you're gon-na miss me when_ I'm gone, _____

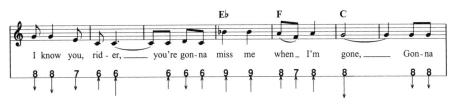

I know you, rid - er, _____ you're gon-na miss me when_ I'm gone, _____ Gon - na

miss your lit - tle mom-ma from a - roll - ing in _____ your arms. _____

I'm goin' down the road where I can get more decent care,
I'm goin' down the road where I can get more decent care,
Goin' back to my used-to-be rider 'cause I don't feel welcome here.

I know my baby sure is bound to love me, some,
I know my baby sure is bound to love me, some,
'Cause he throws his arms around me like a circle 'round the sun.

I laid down last night tryin' to take a rest,
I laid down last night tryin' to take a rest,
But my mind kept rambling like the wild geese in the West.

I'm goin' down to the river, set in my rocking chair,
I'm goin' down to the river, set in my rocking chair,
And if the blues don't find me, gonna rock away from here.

Lovin' you, baby, just as easy as rollin' off a log,
Lovin' you, baby, just as easy as rollin' off a log,
But if I can't be your woman, I sure ain't gonna be your dog.

Sun gonna shine in my back yard some day,
Sun gonna shine in my back yard some day,
And the wind gonna rise up, baby, blow my blues away.

Jelly Roll Blues

E Harmonica

I'm like a one-eyed cat now, peepin' in a seafood store,
I'm like a one-eyed cat now, peepin' in a seafood store,
Little taste of your sweet thing, now, you know I'll be back for more.

Well, it's jelly, jelly, jelly, 'cause jelly stays on my mind,
Well, it's jelly, jelly, jelly, 'cause jelly stays on my mind,
It might be your sweet thing, I'm gonna use it sometime.

Well, I got nineteen women livin' in my neighborhood,
Well, I got nineteen women livin' in my neighborhood,
Eighteen are fools and the other one's no damn good.

I got a big fat mama lays steel down on the track,
I got a big fat mama lays steel down on the track,
When that mama loves me it almost breaks my back.

Don't you wish you had a big, fat mama like mine?
Don't you wish you had a big, fat mama like mine?
Her knees stick out in front, and her calves way out behind.

You got bad blood, baby, I think you need a shot,
You got bad blood, baby, I think you need a shot,
On your back now, baby, let the doctor see what else you got.

I'm gonna sing this verse an' I ain't gonna sing it no more,
I'm gonna sing this verse an' I ain't gonna sing it no more,
Put your man in bed, your husband down on the floor.

Joe Turner

C Harmonica

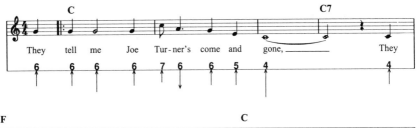

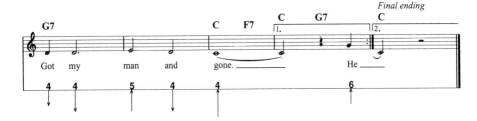

He come with forty links of chain,
He come with forty links of chain (Oh, Lordy),
Got my man and gone.

They tell me Joe Turner's come and gone,
They tell me Joe Turner's come and gone, (Oh, Lordy),
Done left me here to sing this song.

Come like he never come before,
Come like he never come before, (Oh, Lordy),
Got my man and gone.

Mule Skinner Blues

E Harmonica

Well, I like to work - I'm rolling all the time,
Yes, I like to work - I'm rolling all the time,
I can pop my initials right on the mule's behind.

Well, it's hey, little water boy, bring your water 'round,
Hey, little water boy, bring your water 'round,
If you don't like your job set that water bucket down.

I'm a-working on the new road at a dollar and a dime a day,
Working on that new road at a dollar and a dime a day,
I got three women waiting on a Saturday night just to draw my pay.

Number Twelve Train

A Harmonica

She left me all night long, I could not help myself,
She left me all night long, I could not help myself,
I thought she was loving me - I found she had somebody else.

I may be wrong, but I'll be right some day,
I may be wrong, but I'll be right some day,
But the next gal I get will have to do what poppa say.

Sportin' Life Blues

G Harmonica

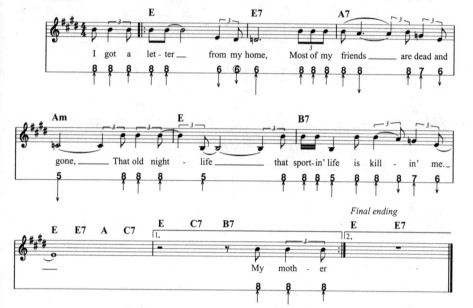

My mother used to say to me,
So young and foolish, that I can't see,
Ain't got no mother, my sister and brother won't talk to me.

I've been a liar and a cheater too,
Spent all my money on booze and you,
That old night life, that sportin' life is killin' me.

My mother used to say to me,
So young and foolish, that I can't see,
Ho, Jerry, hey there, Jerry, why don't you change your ways?

I've been a gambler and a cheater too,
But now it's come my turn to lose,
That old sportin' life has got the best hand, what can I do?

There ain't but one thing that I've done wrong,
Lived this sportin' life, my friend, too long,
I say it's no good, please believe me, please leave it alone.

I'm gettin' tired of runnin' 'round,
Think I will marry and settle down,
That old night life, that sportin' life is killin' me.

St. James Infirmary

C Harmonica

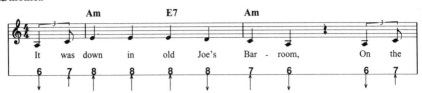

It was down in old Joe's Bar - room, On the
6 7 8 8 8 8 7 6 6 7

cor - ner by the square, The ___ drinks were served as
8 8 10 9 8 6 7 8 8 8 8

u - sual, And the u - su - al ___ crowd ___ was there. ___
7 6 6 7 7 6 7 6 8 8 7 6

On my left stood big Joe McKennedy,
His eyes were bloodshot red,
He turned to the crowd around him,
These were the very words he said.

"I went down to the St. James Infirmary
"To see my baby there,
"She was stretched out on a long white table,
"So pale, so cold and so fair."

Let her go, let her go, God bless her,
Wherever she may be,
She may search this whole world over,
Never find a man as sweet as me.

When I die, please bury me
In my high-top Stetson hat,
Put a twenty-dollar gold piece on my watch chain,
So the gang'll know I died standing pat.

I want six crap shooters for pall bearers,
Six pretty gals to sing me a song,
Put a jazz band on my hearse wagon,
To raise hell as we stroll along.

And now that you've heard my story,
I'll have another shot of booze,
And if anybody happens to ask you,
I've got the St. James Infirmary blues.

Take Your Fingers Off It

Each verse begins with the same 8 measures as the first.

Take your fingers off it. . .
Two old maids a-layin' in bed,
One turned over toward the other and said,
Take your fingers off it, and don't you dare touch it,
You know it don't belong to you.

Take your fingers off it. . .
A nickel is a nickel, a dime is a dime,
A house full of children none of them's mine.
Take your fingers off it, and don't you dare touch it,
You know it don't belong to you.

Take your fingers off it. . .
Saddest day ever in my life,
When I caught my best friend a-kissing my wife.
Take your fingers off it and don't you dare touch it,
You know it don't belong to you.

Things About Comin' My Way

E Harmonica

The pot was empty, the cupboard bare,
I said, "Mama, mama, what's goin' on here?" *Chorus*

The rent was due, the light was out,
I said, "Mama, mama, what's it all about?" *Chorus*

Sister was sick, doc wouldn't come
'Cause we couldn't pay him the proper sum. *Chorus*

Lost all my money, ain't got a dime,
Givin' up this cold world, leavin' it behind. *Chorus*

Work all this summer and all the fall,
Gonna make this Christmas in my overalls. *Chorus*

One of these days - it won't be long,
You'll call my name and I'll be gone.

Final Chorus:

'Cause after all my hard trav'lin',
Things'll be comin' my way.

Wanderin'

C Harmonica

My dad-dy is an en-gi-neer, my broth-er drives a hack, My

6   7   7   7   7   7   7   7   7   7   7   7   7   7

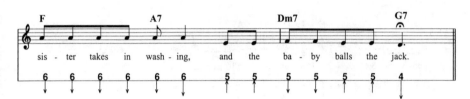

sis - ter takes in wash - ing, and the ba - by balls the jack.

6   6   6   6   6   6   5   5   5   5   5   5   4

Chorus

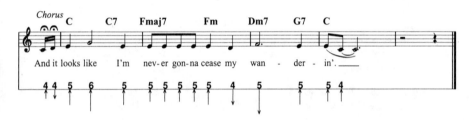

And it looks like I'm nev-er gon-na cease my wan - der - in'.____

4 4   5   6   5   5 5 5 5 5   4   5   5   5 4

I've been a-wanderin' early and late,
New York City to the Golden Gate. *Chorus*

Been a-workin' in the city; been a-workin' on the farm,
And all I've got to show for it is the muscle in my arm. *Chorus*

Snakes in the ocean, eels in the sea,
A redheaded woman made a fool out of me. *Chorus*

Winnsboro Cotton Mill Blues

When I die, don't bury me at all,
Just hang me up on the spool room wall,
Place a knotter in my hand,
So I can spool in the promised land. *Chorus*

When I die, don't bury me deep,
Bury me down on Six Hundred Street,
Place a bobbin in each hand,
So I can dolph in the promised land. *Chorus*

Alberta, Let Your Hair Hang Low

C Harmonica

Alberta, what's on your mind?
Alberta, what's on your mind?
You keep me worried, bothered all the time.
Alberta, what's on your mind?

Alberta, don'cha treat me unkind.
Alberta, don'cha treat me unkind.
Oh, my heart is sad 'cause I want you so bad.
Alberta, don'cha treat me unkind.

Believe Me, If All Those Endearing Young Charms

C Harmonica

Thomas Moore

Ireland

It is not while beauty and youth are thine own,
And thy cheeks unprofaned by a tear;
But the fervor and faith of a soul can be known,
To which time will but make thee more dear.

Oh, the heart that has truly loved never forgets,
But as truly loves on to the close
As the sunflower turns on her god when he sets
The same look that she gave when he rose.

Blow the Candles Out

C Harmonica

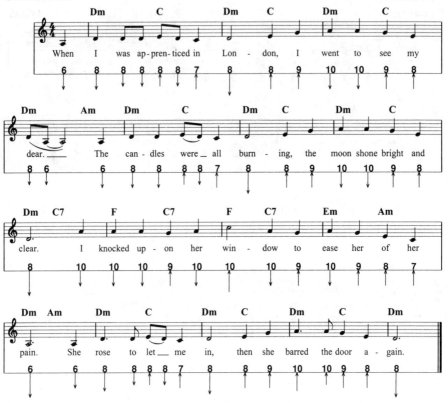

I like your well behaviour and thus I often say,
I cannot rest contented whilst you are far away.
The roads they are so muddy, we cannot gang about,
So roll me in your arms, love, and blow the candles out.

Your father and your mother in yonder room do lie,
A-huggin' one another, so why not you and I?
A-huggin' one another without fear or doubt,
So roll me in your arms, love, and blow the candles out.

And if you prove successful, love, pray name it after me,
Keep it neat and kiss it sweet, and daff it on your knee,
When my three years are ended, my time will be out,
Then I will double my indebtedness by blowing the candles out.

Careless Love

E Harmonica

I cried last night and the night before,
I cried last night and the night before,
I cried last night and the night before,
Gonna cry tonight and cry no more.

I love my mama and my papa too,
I love my mama and my papa too,
I love my mama and my papa too,
But I'd leave them both to go with you.

When I wore my apron low,
When I wore my apron low,
When I wore my apron low,
You'd follow me through rain and snow.

Now I wear my apron high,
Now I wear my apron high,
Now I wear my apron high,
You see my door and pass on by.

How I wish that train would come,
How I wish that train would come,
How I wish that train would come,
And take me back where I come from.

Repeat first verse

Cindy

E Harmonica

Oh, have you seen my Cin - dy? She comes from 'way down south, And she's so sweet, the hon - ey bees just swarm a - round her mouth.

Chorus

Get a - long home, Cin - dy, Cin - dy, Get a - long home, Cin - dy, Cin - dy, Get a - long home, Cin - dy, Cin - dy, I'll mar - ry you some day.

I wish I was an apple,
A-hangin' in a tree,
And ev'ry time my sweetheart passed,
She'd take a bite of me. *Chorus*

She told me that she loved me,
She called me sugar plum,
She throwed 'er arms around me,
I thought my time had come. *Chorus*

She took me to the parlor,
She cooled me with her fan.
She swore I was the purtiest thing
In the shape of mortal man. *Chorus*

I wish I had a needle,
As fine as I could sew;
I'd sew the girls to my coat tail,
And down the road I'd go. *Chorus*

Cindy got religion,
She had it once before;
But when she heard my old banjo,
She 'uz the first un on the floor. *Chorus*

Cindy went to the preachin',
She swung around and around;
She got so full of glory,
She knocked preacher down. *Chorus*

Come, All Ye Fair and Tender Ladies

G Harmonica

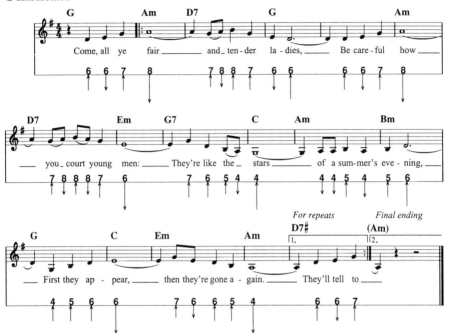

They'll tell to you some loving story,
They'll declare to you their love is true;
Straightway they'll go and court some other,
And that's the love they have for you.

I wish I was some little sparrow,
That I had wings and I could fly;
I'd fly away to my false true lover,
And when he's talking I'd be nigh.

But I am not a little sparrow,
And neither have I wings to fly;
I'll sit down here in grief and sorrow
To weep and pass my troubles by.

If I'd a-known before I courted,
I never would have courted none;
I'd have locked my heart in a box of golden,
And pinned it up with a silver pin.

Don't Sing Love Songs

A Harmonica

"All men are false," says my mother,
"They'll tell you wicked, lovely lies,
And the very next evening, court another
Leaving you alone to pine and sigh."

My father is a handsome devil,
He's got a chain that's five miles long,
And every link a heart does dangle
Of some poor maid he's loved and wronged.

Wish that I was some little sparrow,
Yes, one of those that flies so high,
I'd fly away to my false true lover,
And when he'd speak I would deny.

On his breast, I'd light and flutter
With my little tender wings,
I'd ask him who he meant to flatter,
Or who he meant to deceive.

Go court some other tender lady,
And I hope that she will be your wife,
'Cause I've been warned and I've decided
To sleep alone all my life.

Down by the Sally Gardens

C Harmonica

William Butler Yeats

Ireland

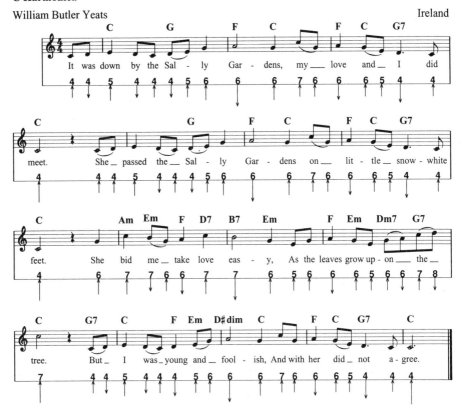

In a field by the river,
My love and I did stand.
Upon my leaning shoulder
She placed her snow-white hand.
She bid me take life easy,
As the grass grows on the weirs.
But I was young and foolish,
And now am full of tears.

The Foggy, Foggy Dew

G Harmonica

One night she knelt close by my side
As I lay fast asleep.
She threw her arms around my neck,
And then began to weep.
She wept, she cried, she tore her hair,
Ah, me, what could I do?
So all night long I held her in my arms
Just to keep her from the foggy, foggy dew.

Oh, I am a bachelor, I live with my son,
We work at the weaver's trade.
And every single time I look into his eyes
He reminds me of the fair young maid.
He reminds me of the wintertime,
And of the summer too.
And the many, many times I held her in my arms
Just to keep her from the foggy, foggy dew.

Frankie and Johnny

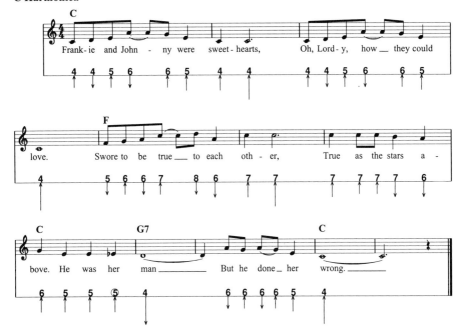

C Harmonica

Frank-ie and John - ny were sweet-hearts, Oh, Lord- y, how __ they could love. Swore to be true __ to each oth - er, True as the stars a - bove. He was her man __ But he done __ her wrong. ____

Frankie and Johnny went walking,
Johnny in his brand-new suit.
"Oh, good Lord," said Frankie,
"Don't my Johnny man look cute?"
He was her man, but he done her wrong.

Johnny said, "I've got to leave you,
But I won't be very long.
Don't wait up for me, honey,
Or worry while I'm gone."
He was her man, but he done her wrong.

Frankie went down to the corner
To get a bucket of beer.
She said to the fat bartender,
"Has my lovin' man been here?"
He was her man, but he done her wrong.

"Well, I ain't gonna tell you a story,
I ain't gonna tell you no lie.
I saw your Johnny 'bout an hour ago
With a gal named Nellie Bly."
He was her man, but he done her wrong.

Oh, Frankie got off at South Twelfth Street,
Looked up in a window so high,
And there she saw her Johnny
A-huggin' that Nellie Bly.
He was her man, but he done her wrong.

Frankie pulled out her six-shooter,
Pulled out her old forty-four.
Her gun went rooty-toot-toot-toot,
And Johnny rolled over the floor.
He was her man, but he done her wrong.

Roll out your rubber-tired carriage,
Roll out your old-time hack.
There's twelve men goin' to the graveyard,
And eleven coming back.
He was her man, but he done her wrong.

"Oh, roll me over so easy,
Oh, roll me over so slow.
Oh, roll me over easy, boys,
For my wounds, they hurt me so -
I was her man, but I done her wrong."

Frankie got down on her knees,
Took Johnny into her lap.
She started to hug and kiss him,
But there was no bringing him back.
He was her man, but he done her wrong.

"Oh, get me a thousand policemen,
Oh, throw me into your cell,
'Cause I've shot my Johnny so dead,
I know I'm going to hell."
He was her man, but he done her wrong.

Gently, Johnny, My Jingalo

G Harmonica

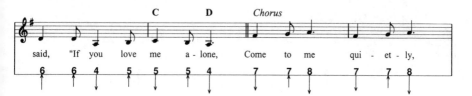

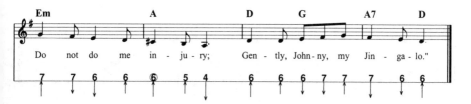

I said, "You know, I love you, dear."
  Fair maid is a lily, O.
She whispered softly in my ear. *Chorus*

I placed my arm around her waist.
  Fair maid is a lily, O.
She laughed and turned away her face. *Chorus*

I kissed her lips like rubies red.
  Fair maid is a lily, O.
She blushed, then tenderly she said. *Chorus*

I slipped a ring all in her hand.
  Fair maid is a lilly, O.
She said, "The parson's near at hand." *Chorus*

I took her to the church next day.
  Fair maid is a lily, O.
The birds did sing and she did say. *Chorus*

Greensleeves

Thy smock of gold so crimson red,
With pearls bedecked sumptuously.
The like no other lasses had,
And yet thou wouldest not love me. *Chorus*

Thy gown was of the grassy green,
Thy sleeves of satin hanging by;
Which made thee be our harvest queen,
And yet thou wouldest not love me. *Chorus*

Thou couldst desire no earthly thing,
But still thou hadst it readily;
Thy music still to play and sing,
And yet thou wouldest not love me. *Chorus*

Well, I will pray to God on high
That thou my constancy mayst see;
And that yet once before I die
Thou wilt vouchsafe to love me. *Chorus*

Greensleeves, now farewell, adieu!
God I pray to prosper thee;
For I am still thy lover true -
Come once again and love me. *Chorus*

He's Gone Away

C Harmonica

I'm goin' a - way for to stay a lit - tle while, But I'm
4 6   6 8   8 8 8   7 7 6 6   6 7

com - ing back, if I go ten thou - sand miles; Oh, who will tie your
8 8   7   6 6 7   6 6 ⑤ 4   4   6   6   7   6

shoes? And who will glove your hand? And who will kiss those ru - by
6   6   7   8 9   8   8   6   7   8   ⑨ 8 8 8

lips when I am gone? Look a - way, look a - way o - ver Yan - dro.
8 7   6 ⑤ 4   5 4 6   5 4 6   7 6 7 6

He's gone away for to stay a little while,
But he's coming back if he goes ten thousand miles.
Oh, it's daddy'll tie my shoes.
And mommy'll glove my hands,
And you will kiss my ruby lips when you come back!
Look away, look away over Yandro.

How Should I Your True Love Know

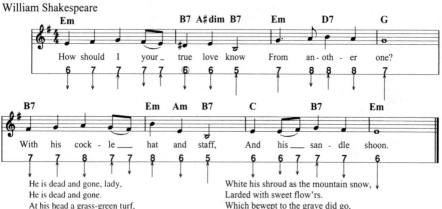

G Harmonica

William Shakespeare

How should I your _ true love know From an - oth - er one?
6   7   7 7 7   ⑥ 6 5   7   8 8   8   7

With his cock - le _ hat and staff, And his _ san - dle shoon.
7   7   8   7 7   8   6 5   6   6 7 7   7   6

He is dead and gone, lady,   White his shroud as the mountain snow,
He is dead and gone.   Larded with sweet flow'rs.
At his head a grass-green turf,   Which bewept to the grave did go,
At his head a stone.   With true love show'rs.

Hurree Hurroo

D Harmonica .

Scotland (Hebrides)

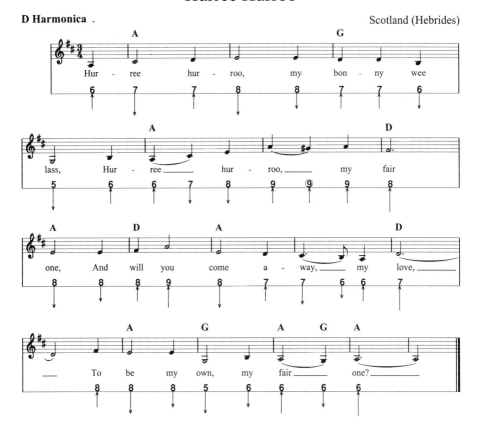

Smiling the land, smiling the sea,
Sweet was the smell of the heather.
Would we were yonder, just you and me,
The two of us together. *Chorus*

All the day long out by the peat,
Then by the shore in the gloaming.
Tripping it lightly with dancing feet,
Then we together roaming. *Chorus*

I'll Give My Love an Apple

C Harmonica

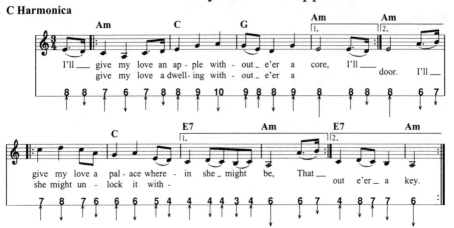

How can there be an apple without e'er a core?
How can there be a dwelling without e'er a door?
How can there be a palace wherein she might be,
That she might unlock it without e'er a key?

My head is the apple without e'er a core,
My mind is the dwelling without e'er a door.
My heart is the palace wherein she might be,
That she might unlock it without e'er a key.

I'm Sad and I'm Lonely

A Harmonica

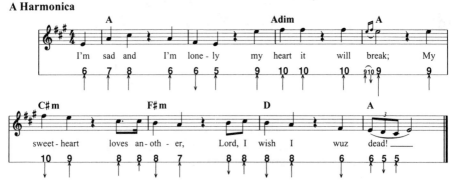

Young ladies take warning,
Take warning from me,
Don't waste your affections
On a young man so free.

He'll hug you and he'll kiss you
And he'll tell you more lies
Than the cross-ties on the railroad
Or the stars in the sky.

My cheeks once were red
Like the red, red rose;
But now they are white
As the lily that grows.

I'll build me a cabin
On the mountain so high,
Where the blackbirds can't find me
Or hear my sad cry.

I'm troubled, yes, I'm troubled.
I'm troubled, in my mind,
If this trouble don't kill me,
I'll live a long time.

John Riley

C Harmonica

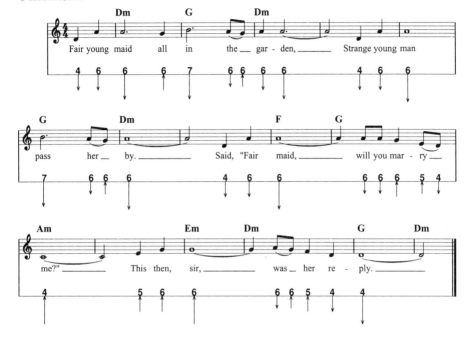

Fair young maid all in the gar - den, Strange young man pass her by. Said, "Fair maid, will you mar - ry me?" This then, sir, was her re - ply.

"Oh no, kind sir, I cannot marry,
For I've a love who sails the sea.
He's been gone for these seven years.
Still no man shall marry me."

"What if he's in battle slain?
Or drowned in the deep salt sea?
What if he's found another love,
And that they both married be?"

"If he's in some battle slain,
I'll die when the moon doth wane.
If he's drowned in the deep salt sea,
I'll be true to his memory."

"If he's found another love,
And if they both married be.
Then I wish them happiness,
Where they dwell across the sea."

He picked her up all in his arms,
Kisses gave her, one, two, three.
"Weep no more, my own true love,
I'm your long lost John Riley."

Lily of the West

C Harmonica

When first I came to Lou-is - ville, _____ Some pleas-ure there to
find. _____ A dam-sel there from Lex-ing-ton ___ was pleas-ing to my
mind. _____ Her ros - y cheeks, her ru - by lips, ___ like ar - rows pierced my
breast, ___ And the name she bore was Flo - ra, _____ the Lil - y of the West. ___

I courted lovely Flora some pleasure
  there to find,
But she turned unto another man which
  sore distressed my mind.
She robbed me of my liberty, deprived
  me of my rest,
Then go my love Flora, the Lily of
  the West.

Way down in yonder shady grove, a
  man of high degree,
Conversing with my Flora there, it
  seemed so strange to me.
And the answer that she gave to him, it
  sore did me oppress,
I was betrayed by Flora, the Lily of
  the West.

I stepped up to my rival, my dagger in
  my hand,
I seized him by the collar and I boldly
  bade him stand.
Being mad to desperation I pierced
  him in the breast.
Then go my lovely Flora, the Lily of
  the West.

I had to stand my trial, I had to make
  my plea,
They placed me in a criminal box and
  then commenced on me.
Although she swore my life away,
  deprived me of my rest,
Still I love my faithless Flora, the
  Lily of the West.

Malagueña Salerosa

C Harmonica   Mexico

What beautiful eyes you have... but you don't look at me... I want to kiss your lips... If you spurn me
because I am poor... I offer you my heart instead of my poverty... I want to kiss your lips...

Si por pobre me desprecias
Yo te concedo razón,
Yo te concedo razón,
Si por pobre me desprecias.

Yo no te ofresco riqueza.
Te ofresco mi corazón,
Te ofresco mi corazón,
En cambio de mi pobreza. *Chorus*

Maple Leaf Rag

A Harmonica
Sydney Brown

Scott Joplin

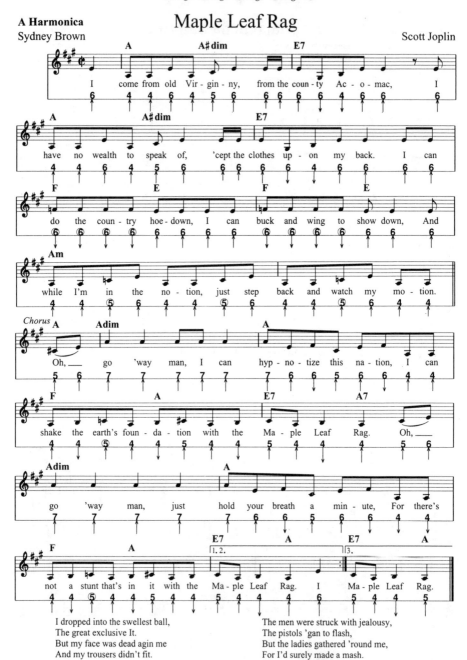

I dropped into the swellest ball,
The great exclusive It.
But my face was dead agin me
And my trousers didn't fit.
But when Maple Leaf was started,
My timidity departed.
I lost my trepidation,
You could taste the admiration. *Chorus*

The men were struck with jealousy,
The pistols 'gan to flash.
But the ladies gathered 'round me,
For I'd surely made a mash.
The finest belle she sent a boy
To call a coach and pair.
We rode around a season
Till we both were lost to reason. *Chorus*

Moscow Nights

C Harmonica

M. Matusovskii
English lyrics by Jerry Silverman

V. Solovyov-Sedoi

Still - ness in the grove not a rust - ling sound. Soft - ly shines the
Nye slysh - ny v sa - du da - zhe sho - ro - khi. Vsyo zdyes za - mer -

6 7 8 7 8 7 7 8 8 6 7 8 9 8

moon clear and bright. Dear, if you could know _____ how I
lo do oo - tra Yes - li b zna - li - vy _____ kak mnye

10 9 9 8 9 10 10 10 8 7 6

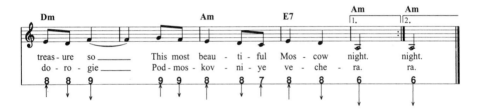

treas - ure so _____ This most beau - ti - ful Mos - cow night. night.
do - ro - gie _____ Pod - mos - kov - ni - ye ve - che - ra. ra.

8 8 9 9 9 8 8 7 8 8 6 6

Lazily the brook, like a silv'ry stream,
Ripples gently in the moonlight;
And a song afar fades as in a dream
In the spell of this summer night. *(2 times)*

Dearest, why so sad, why the downcast eyes,
And your lovely head bent so low?
Oh, it's hard to speak - and yet not to speak
Of the longing my heart does know. *(2 times)*

Promise me, my love, as the dawn appears,
And the darkness turns into light,
That you'll cherish, dear, through the passing years,
This most beautiful Moscow night. *(2 times)*

Rechka dvizhetsia i nye dvizhetsia.
Vsia iz lunnovo serebra.
Pyesnia slyshitsia i nye slyshitsia
V eti tikhiye vechera. *(2 times)*

Chto zh ty milaia smotrish iskosa,
Nizko golovu naklonia?
Trudno vyskazat i nye vyskazat
Vsyo, chto na serdtse oo menia. *(2 times)*

A rassvyet oozhe vsyo zametneya...
Tak, pozhaluista, bood dobra.
Nye zabood i ty eti letniye
Podmoskovniye vechera. *(2 times)*

❁ ❁ ❁ ❁ ❁ ❁ ❁ ❁ ❁

Plaisir d'Amour

This song changes key. To play it properly, you will need two harmonicas, D and F (or E, G; A, C).

Jean Paul Martini
(1741 - 1816)
France

D Harmonica

Section I

Plai - sir d'a - mour ____ ne du - re qu'un __ mo - ment; ____ cha - grin d'a - mour du - re tou - te la vi - e. J'ai e. *Change to F harmonica* e.

1. To Section II
2. To Section III
3. Final ending

Section II

tout quit - té pour l'in - gra - te Syl - vi - e; ____ el - le me quit - te et prend __ un au - tre a - mant. Plai-

Return to sign 𝄋 until Ending 2

F Harmonica

Section III

"Tant que cet - te eau cou - le - ra dou - ce - ment ____ vers ce ruis - seau qui bor - de la __ prai - ri - e je t'ai - me - rai." Me ré - pé - tait __ Syl -

D. S. 𝄋 to Final Ending (Ending 3)

vi - e. L'eau cou - le en - core, ____ el - le a chan - gé pour - tant. ____ Plai-

Change to D harmonica

Scarborough Fair

G Harmonica

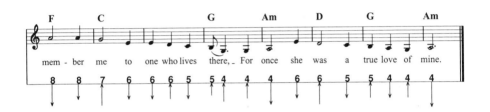

Man's lyrics

Tell her to make me a cambric shirt,
Parsley, sage, rosemary and thyme.
Without any seam or fine needlework.
And then she'll be a true love of mine.

Tell her to wash it in yonder dry well,
Parsley, sage, rosemary and thyme.
Where water ne'er sprung, nor drop of rain fell,
And then she'll be a true love of mine.

Tell her to dry it on yonder thorn,
Parsley, sage, rosemary and thyme.
Which never bore blossom since Adam was born,
And then she'll be a true love of mine.

Woman's lyrics

Will you find me an acre of land,
Parsley, sage, rosemary and thyme.
Between the sea foam and the sea sand.
Or never be a true love of mine.

Will you plough it with a lamb's horn,
Parsley, sage, rosemary and thyme.
And sow it all over with one peppercorn,
Or never be a true love of mine.

Will you reap it with sickle of leather,
Parsley, sage, rosemary and thyme.
And tie it all up with a peacock's feather,
Or never be a true love of mine.

When you've done and finished your work,
Parsley, sage, rosemary and thyme.
Then come to me for your cambric shirt,
And you shall be a true love of mine.

She Moved Through the Fair

G Harmonica

Ireland

She stepped away from me
And she went through the fair,
And fondly I watched her move here and move there.
And then she went homeward
With one star awake,
As the swan in the evening moves over the lake.

Last night she came to me,
She came softly in.
So softly she came that her feet made no din.
And she laid her hand on me,
And this she did say,
"It will not be long, love, till our wedding day."

The Water is Wide

C Harmonica

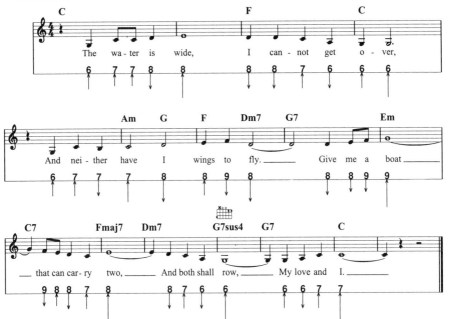

A ship there is and she sails the sea,
She's loaded deep as deep can be.
But not so deep as the love I'm in,
And I know not how to sink or swim.

I leaned my back against a young oak,
Thinking he was a trusty tree.
But first he bended and then he broke,
And thus did my false love to me.

I put my hand into some soft bush,
Thinking the sweetest flower to find.
The thorn, it stuck me to the bone,
And, oh, I left that flower alone.

Oh, love is handsome and love is fine,
Gay as a jewel when first it's new.
But love grows old and waxes cold,
And fades away like summer dew.

Who's Gonna Shoe Your Pretty Little Foot?

C Harmonica

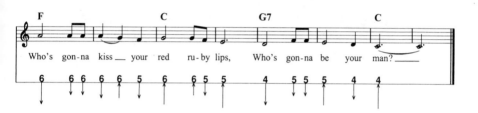

Who's gonna be your man,
Who's gonna be your man,
Who's gonna kiss your red ruby lips,
Who's gonna be your man?

Well, papa's gonna shoe my pretty little foot,
Mama's gonna glove my hand,
And sister's gonna kiss my red ruby lips,
I don't need no man.

I don't need no man,
I don't need no man,
Sister's gonna kiss my red ruby lips,
I don't need no man.

The longest train I ever did see
Was a hundred coaches long,
The only woman I ever did love
Was on that train and gone.

On that train and gone,
On that train and gone,
The only woman I ever did love
Was on that train and gone.

Brown's Ferry Blues

A Harmonica

Hard luck pop - pa count - ing his toes, You can smell his feet where -
Hard luck pop - pa done lost his stuff, The trou - ble is he's

ev - er he goes. Lord, Lord, got those Brown's Fer - ry blues.
played too rough.

Brown's Fer - ry blues.

Two old maids a-sitting in the sand,
Each one wishing that the other was a man,
Lord, Lord, got those Brown's Ferry blues.
Two old maids done lost their style,
If you want to be lucky you got to smile,
Lord, Lord, got those Brown's Ferry blues.

Early to bed and early to rise,
And your girl goes out with other guys,
Lord, Lord, got those Brown's Ferry blues.
If you don't believe me try it yourself,
Well I tried it and I got left,
Lord, Lord, got those Brown's Ferry blues.

Hard luck poppa standin' in the rain,
If the world was corn he couldn't buy grain,
Lord, Lord, got those Brown's Ferry blues.
Hard luck poppa standin' in the snow,
His knees knock together but he's raring to go,
Lord, Lord, got those Brown's Ferry blues.

Bury Me Beneath the Willow

E Harmonica

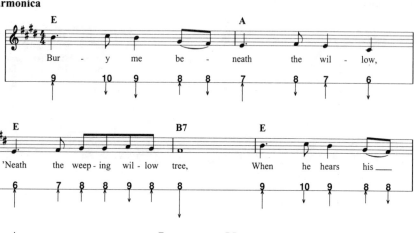

My heart is sad and I am lonely,
Thinking of one I love,
When will I meet him? Oh, no never,
Unless we meet in heaven above.

Tomorrow was to be our wedding,
I pray, Oh Lord, where can he be,
He's gone, he's gone to love some other;
He no longer cares for me.

He told me that he dearly loved me,
How could I believe him untrue,
Until one day some neighbors told me,
"He has proven untrue to you."

Repeat first verse

Crawdad

E Harmonica

Get up, old man, you slept too late, honey,
Get up, old man, you slept too late, baby,
Get up, old man, you slept too late,
Last piece of crawdad's on your plate,
 Honey, sugar baby, mine.

Get up, old woman, you slept too late, honey,
Get up, old woman, you slept too late, baby,
Get up, old woman, you slept too late,
Crawdad man done passed your gate,
 Honey, sugar baby, mine.

Along come a man with a sack on his back, honey,
Along come a man with a sack on his back, baby,
Along come a man with a sack on his back,
Packing all the crawdads he can pack,
 Honey, sugar baby, mine.

What you gonna do when the lake goes dry, honey?
What you gonna do when the lake goes dry, baby?
What you gonna do when the lake goes dry?
Sit on the bank and watch the crawdads die,
 Honey, sugar baby, mine.

D Harmonica

Cripple Creek

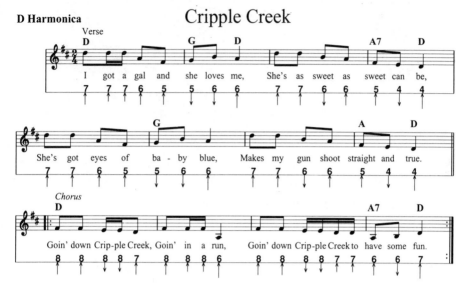

Verse

I got a gal and she loves me, She's as sweet as sweet can be,
7 7 7 6 5 5 6 6 7 7 6 6 5 4 4

She's got eyes of ba - by blue, Makes my gun shoot straight and true.
7 7 6 5 5 6 6 7 7 6 6 5 4 4

Chorus

Goin' down Crip-ple Creek, Goin' in a run, Goin' down Crip-ple Creek to have some fun.
8 8 8 8 7 8 8 8 6 8 8 8 8 7 7 6 6 7

I got a beau and he loves me,
He's as sweet as sweet can be,
He's got eyes of darkest brown,
Makes my heart jump all around. *Chorus*

Goin' down to Cripple Creek fast as I can go,
Goin' down to Cripple Creek, don't be slow,
Raise my britches above my knees,
Wade in Cripple Creek if I please. *Chorus*

C Harmonica

Cumberland Gap

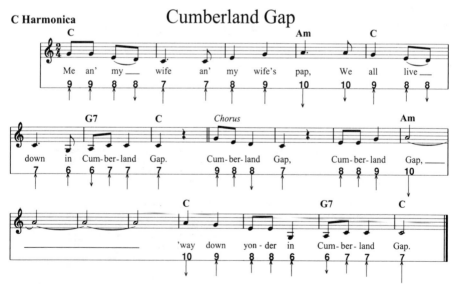

Me an' my ___ wife an' my wife's pap, We all live ___
9 9 8 8 7 7 8 9 10 10 9 8 8

down in Cum-ber-land Gap. Cum-ber-land Gap, Cum-ber-land Gap, ___
7 6 6 7 7 9 8 8 7 8 8 9 10

Chorus

___ 'way down yon-der in Cum-ber-land Gap.
10 9 8 8 6 6 7 7 7

Cumberland Gap is a noted place,
Three kinds of water to wash your face. *Chorus*

The first white man in Cumberland Gap
Was Doctor Walker, an English chap. *Chorus*

Daniel Boone on Pinnacle Rock,
He killed bears with his old flintlock. *Chorus*

Lay down, boys, and take a little nap.
Fourteen miles to the Cumberland Gap. *Chorus*

Darling Cory

A Harmonica

Wake up, wake up, Dar-ling Cor-y, What

makes you sleep so sound? The rev-e-nue of-fi-cers are

com-ing For to tear your still-house down.

The first time I see Darling Cory,
She was standing on the banks of the sea,
She had a pistol strapped 'round her bosom
And a banjo on her knee.

Go 'way from me, Darling Cory,
Quit hanging 'round my bed,
Pretty women have run me distracted,
Corn likker's gone to my head.

Oh, no, oh, no my darling,
I'll do the best I can,
I'll get me another woman -
You can hunt you another man.

Dig a hole, dig a hole in the meadow,
A hole in the cold, cold ground,
Go and dig me a hole in the meadow,
For to lay Darling Cory down.

Don't Let Your Deal Go Down

A Harmonica

Well, I've been all around this whole wide world,
Done 'most everything,
Well, I've played cards with the king and queen,
The ace, the duece and the trey. *Chorus*

Where did you get that bright red dress,
And the shoes that you wear so fine?
I got my dress and I got my shoes
From a driver down in the mine. *Chorus*

I left my little girl a-cryin',
Standing in the door,
She threw her arms all around my neck,
Saying, "Honey, please don't go." *Chorus*

E Harmonica

Foggy Mountain Top

Oh, she's caused me to weep and she's caused me to moan,
She caused me to leave my home;
The lonesome pines and the good old times,
I'm on my way back home. *Chorus*

Oh, if I'd only listened to what my mama said,
I would not have been here today,
Lying around this old jail cell,
Just a-weeping my poor life away. *Chorus*

Freight Train

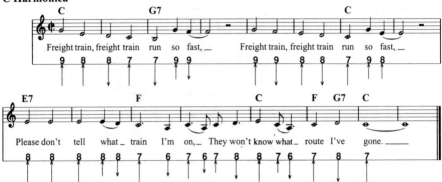

C Harmonica

Freight train, freight train run so fast, __ Freight train, freight train run so fast, __

Please don't tell what _ train I'm on, __ They won't know what _ route I've gone. ____

When I am dead and in my grave,
No more good times here I'll crave,
Place the stones at my head and feet,
And tell them all that I'm gone to sleep.

When I die, Lord, bury me deep,
Way down on old Chestnut Street,
So I can hear old Number Nine
As she comes rolling by.

When I die, Lord, bury me deep,
Way down on old Chestnut Street,
Place the stones at my head and feet,
And tell them all that I'm gone to sleep.

Repeat first verse

Goin' Across the Mountain

D Harmonica

Goin' a - cross the moun - tain, Oh, fare you well,

Goin' a - cross the moun - tain, You can hear my ban - jo tell.

Got my rations on my back,
My powder, it is dry,
I'm a-goin' across the mountain,
Chrissie, don't you cry.

Goin' across the mountain,
To join the boys in Blue,
When this war is over,
I'll come back to you.

Goin' across the mountain,
If I have to crawl,
To give old Jeff's men
A little of my rifle ball.

Way before it's good daylight,
If nothing happens to me,
I'll be way down yonder
In old Tennessie.

I expect you'll miss me when I'm gone,
But I'm goin' through,
When this war is over,
I'll come back to you.

Goin' across the mountain,
Oh, fare you well,
Goin' across the mountain,
Oh, fare you well.

Hard, Ain't It Hard

C Harmonica

There is a place in this old town,
And that's where my true love hangs around,
And he takes other women down on his knee,
For to tell them what he never does tell me. *Chorus*

Don't go there a-drinking and a-gambling,
Don't go there your sorrows for to drown,
That hard likker place is a low-down disgrace,
It's the meanest damn' place in this town. *Chorus*

The first time I saw my true love,
He was standing in the door,
And the last time I saw his false-hearted face,
He was dead on the bar-room floor. *Chorus*

Jesse James

G Harmonica

It was Robert Ford, that dirty little coward,
I wonder how he does feel,
For he ate of Jesse's bread and he slept in Jesse's bed,
And he laid poor Jesse in his grave. *Chorus*

How the people held their breath when they heard of
Jesse's death,
And wondered how he ever came to die,
It was one of the gang, called Little Robert Ford,
That shot poor Jesse on the sly. *Chorus*

Jesse was a man, a friend to the poor,
He never would see a man suffer pain,
And with his brother Frank he robbed the Chicago bank,
And stopped the Glendale train. *Chorus*

It was on a Wednesday night, the moon was shining
bright,
They stopped the Glendale train,
And the people, they did say for many miles away,
It was robbed by Frank and Jesse James. *Chorus*

They went to a crossing not very far from there,
And there they did the same.
With the agent on his knees, he delivered up the keys
To the outlaws, Frank and Jesse James. *Chorus*

It was on a Saturday night, Jesse was at home,
Talking to his family brave,
Robert Ford came along like a thief in the night
And laid poor Jesse in his grave. *Chorus*

This song was made by Billy Gashade
As soon as the news did arrive,
He said there was no man with the law in his hand
Who could take Jesse James while alive. *Chorus*

John Hardy

F Harmonica

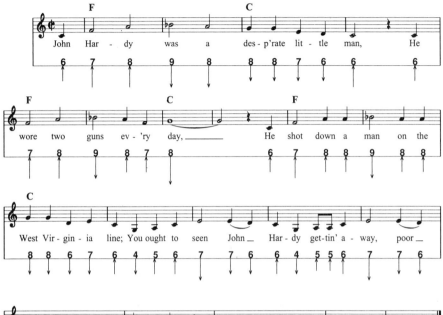

John Har - dy was a des - p'rate lit - tle man, He
wore two guns ev - 'ry day, _____ He shot down a man on the
West Vir - gin - ia line; You ought to seen John __ Har - dy get - tin' a - way, poor __
boy, You ought to seen John __ Har - dy get - tin' a - way. _____

John Hardy stood at the gambling table,
Didn't have no interest in the game,
Up stepped a yellow gal and threw a dollar down,
Said, "John Hardy's playing in my name, poor boy,
John Hardy's playing in my name."

John Hardy took that yellow gal's money,
And then he began to play,
Said, "The man that wins my yellow gal's dollar,
I'll lay him in his lonesome grave, poor boy,
I'll lay him in his lonesome grave."

John Hardy drew to a four-card straight,
And the cowboy drew to a pair,
John failed to catch and the cowboy won,
And he left him sitting dead in his chair, poor boy,
He left him sitting dead in his chair.

John started to catch that east-bound train,
So dark he could not see,
Up stepped the police and took him by the arm,
Said, "Johnny, come and go with me, poor boy,
Johnny, come and go with me."

John Hardy's father came to see him,
Come for to go his bail,
No bail was allowed for a murdering man,
So they shoved John Hardy back in jail, poor boy,
They shoved John Hardy back in jail.

They took John Hardy to the hanging ground,
And hung him there to die,
And the very last words I heard him say
Were, "My forty-four never told a lie, poor boy,
My forty-four never told a lie."

"I've been to the east and I've been to the west,
I've travelled this whole world around,
I've been to the river and I've been baptized,
And now I'm on my hanging ground, poor boy,
Now I'm on my hanging ground."

Listen to the Mockingbird

G Harmonica

Alice Hawthorne

As, well I yet can remember, I remember, I remember,
Ah, well I yet remember
When we gathered in the cotton side by side.
Twas in the mild mid-September, in September, in September,
Twas in the mild mid-September,
And the mockingbird was singing far and wide. *Chorus*

When charms of spring are awaken, are awaken, are
When charms of spring are awaken   awaken,
And the mockingbird is singing on the bough,
I feel like one so forsaken, so forsaken, so forsaken,
I feel like one so forsaken,
Since my Hallie is no longer with me now. *Chorus*

Mountain Dew

E Harmonica

Way up on the hill there's an old whisky still
That is run by a hard-working crew,
You can tell if you sniff and you get a good whiff
That they're making that old mountain dew. *Chorus*

The preacher came by with a tear in his eye,
He said that his wife had the flu,
We told him he ought to give her a quart
Of that good old mountain dew. *Chorus*

My brother Mort is sawed off and short,
He measures just four-foot-two;
But he thinks he's a giant when they give him a pint
Of that good old mountain dew. *Chorus*

My uncle Bill has a still on the hill,
Where he runs off a gallon or two,
The birds in the sky get so high they can't fly,
On that good old mountain dew. *Chorus*

My aunty June has a brand new perfume,
It has such a sweet-smelling pu,
Imagine her surprise when she had it analyzed,
It was good old mountain dew. *Chorus*

Mister Roosevelt told me just how he felt,
The day that the dry law went through:
"If your likker's too red, it will swell up your head,
Better stick to that mountain dew." *Chorus*

❋ ❋ ❋ ❋ ❋ ❋ ❋ ❋

New River Train

C Harmonica

I'm rid-in' on that new riv-er train,   I'm rid-in' on that new riv-er train,

5 6 6 6 6 8 6 6 4   5 6 6 6 6 8 6 6 4

Same old train that brought me here Gon-na car-ry me back a - gain.

4 4 5 5 5 5 6 6 6 6 6 6 5 4 4

Honey, you can't love one,
Honey, you can't love one,
You can't love one and have any fun,
Honey, you can't love one.

Honey, you can't love two,
Honey, you can't love two,
You can't love two and still be true,
Honey, you can't love two.

Honey, you can't love three,
Honey, you can't love three,
You can't love three 'cause you'll be up a tree,
Honey, you can't love three.

Honey, you can't love four,
Honey, you can't love four,
You can't love four or you'll be wanting more,
Honey, you can't love four.

Honey, you can't love five,
Honey, you can't love five,
You can't love five, take them all for a drive,
Honey, you can't love five.

Honey, you can't love six,
Honey, you can't love six,
You can't love six, or you'll be in a fix,
Honey, you can't love six.

Honey, you can't love seven,
Honey, you can't love seven,
You can't love seven and still go to heaven,
Honey, you can't love seven.

Honey, you can't love eight,
Honey, you can't love eight,
You can't love eight and meet them at the gate,
Honey, you can't love eight.

Honey, you can't love nine,
Honey, you can't love nine,
You can't love nine and still be mine,
Honey, you can't love nine.

Honey, you can't love ten,
Honey, you can't love ten,
You can't love ten and sing it all again,
Honey, you can't love ten.

Honey, you must love all,
Honey, you must love all,
You must love all both short and tall,
Honey, you must love all.

91

Pay Day at Coal Creek

G Harmonica

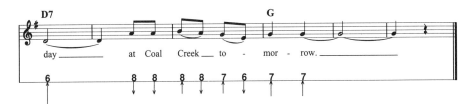

Pay day, pay day, oh, pay day,
Pay day don't come at Coal Creek no more,
Pay day don't come no more.

Bye-bye, bye-bye, oh, bye-bye,
Bye-bye, my woman, I'm gone,
Bye-bye, my woman, I'm gone.

You'll miss me, you'll miss me, you'll miss me,
You'll miss me when I'm gone,
You'll miss me when I'm gone.

I'm a poor boy, I'm a poor boy, I'm a poor boy,
I'm a poor boy and a long ways from home,
I'm a poor boy and a long ways from home.

Easy rider, oh, easy rider, oh, easy rider,
Oh, easy rider, but you'll leave the rail sometime,
Oh, easy rider, but you'll leave the rail sometime.

Pay day, pay day, oh, pay day,
Pay day don't come at Coal Creek no more,
Pay day don't come no more.

Poor Howard

D Harmonica

Poor How - ard's dead and gone, Left me here to sing this song.

sing this song. Poor How - ard's dead and gone,

Poor How - ard's dead and gone,

Left me here to sing this song.

Who's been here since I've been gone?
Pretty little girl with a red dress on.
Who's been here since I've been gone?
Pretty little girl with a red dress on.

Pretty little girl with a red dress on.
Pretty little girl with a red dress on.
Pretty little girl with a red dress on.
Left me here to sing this song.

Who's been here since I've been gone?
Great big man with a derby on.
Who's been here since I've been gone?
Great big man with a derby on.

Great big man with a derby on.
Great big man with a derby on.
Great big man with a derby on.
Left me here to sing this song.

Railroad Bill

C Harmonica

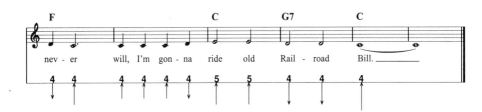

Railroad Bill, he was a mighty mean man,
He shot the midnight lantern out the brakeman's hand,
I'm gonna ride old Railroad Bill.

Railroad Bill took my wife,
Said, if I didn't like it he would take my life,
I'm gonna ride old Railroad Bill.

Going up on the mountain, going out west,
"Thirty-eight special" sticking out of my vest,
I'm gonna ride old Railroad Bill.

I've got a "thirty-eight special" on a "forty-four frame,"
How in the world can I miss him when I've got dead aim,
I'm gonna ride old Railroad Bill.

Buy me a pistol just as long as my arm,
Kill everybody ever done me harm,
I'm gonna ride old Railroad Bill.

Honey, honey, think I'm a fool,
Think I would quit you when the weather is cool?
I'm gonna ride old Railroad Bill.

Rake and Rambling Boy

A Harmonica

Well, _ I'm a rake _____ and a ram - bling _ boy,

5 4 5 6 6   6 6 6 5 4 4

There's man - y a cit - y _____ I did en - joy,

7 7 7 6 7 7   8 8 6 6

And now I mar - ried _____ me a pret - ty lit - tle wife

7 7 6 7 7   7 6 7 7 6 6 6

And I love her dear - er   than I love _ my life. _

5 5 6 6 4 4   5 5 5 4 4 4

My mother said she's all alone,
My sister said she has no home,
My wife she wept in sad despair
With an aching heart and a baby fair.

When I die, don't bury me at all,
Just place me away in alcohol,
My forty-four put by my feet,
Tell everyone I'm just asleep.

Repeat first verse

Red River Valley

D Harmonica

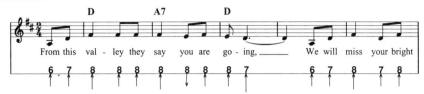

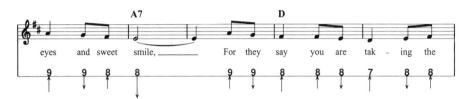

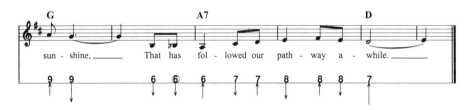

Chorus: Come and sit by my side if you love me,
Do not hasten to bid me adieu,
Just remember the Red River Valley,
And the cowboy who loved you so true.

Won't you think of the valley you're leaving?
Oh, how lonely and sad it will be,
Won't you think of the kind hearts you're breaking,
And the pain you are causing to me? *Chorus*

They will bury me where you have wandered,
Near the hills where the daffodils grow,
When you're gone from the Red River Valley,
For I can't live without you, I know. *Chorus*

Salty Dog

G Harmonica

Salt - y dog, salt - y dog, I don't want to be your man at all.

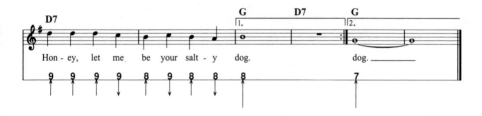

Hon - ey, let me be your salt - y dog. dog. ____

The verses are sung to the first eight measures of the chorus.

Down in the wildwood sitting on a log,
Singing a song about a salty dog.
Honey, let me be your salty dog. *Chorus*

Two old maids a-sitting in the sand,
Each one wishing that the other was a man.
Honey, let me be your salty dog. *Chorus*

Worst day I ever had in my life,
When my best friend caught me kissing his wife.
Honey, let me be your salty dog. *Chorus*

God made a woman and He made her mighty funny,
When you kiss her 'round the mouth just as sweet as any honey.
Honey, let me be your salty dog. *Chorus*

Talking Blues

G Harmonica

No melody-play chords

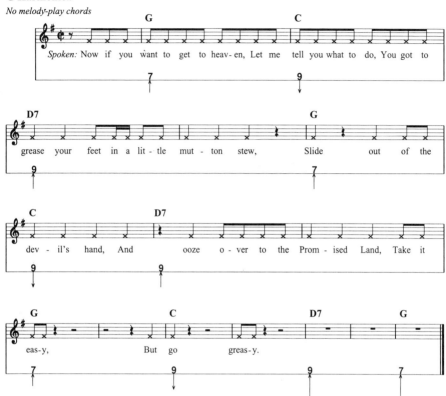

I was down in the holler just a-settin' on a log,
My finger on the trigger and my eye on a hog;
I pulled that trigger and the gun went "zip,"
And I grabbed that hog with all of my grip.
　'Course I can't eat hog eyes, but I love chitlins.

Down in the hen house on my knees,
I thought I heard a chicken sneeze,
But it was only the rooster sayin' his prayers,
Thankin' the Lord for the hens upstairs.
　Rooster prayin', hens a-layin',
　Little pullets just pluggin' away best they know how.

Mama's in the kitchen fixin' the yeast,
Poppa's in the bedroom greasin' his feet,
Sister's in the cellar squeezin' up the hops,
Brother's at the window just a-watchin' for the cops.
　Drinkin' home brew makes you happy.

Now, I'm just a city dude a-livin' out of town,
Everybody knows me as Moonshine Brown;
I make the beer, and I drink the slop,
Got nine little orphans that call me Pop.
　I'm patriotic - raisin' soldiers, Red Cross nurses.

Ain't no use me workin' so hard,
I got a gal in the rich folks' yard,
They kill a chicken, she sends me the head,
She thinks I'm workin', I'm a-layin' up in bed.
　Just dreamin' about her. Havin' a good
　time... two other women...

The Wabash Cannonball

G Harmonica

I stood on the At- lan - tic O - cean, On the wide Pa - ci - fic
long and she's tall and hand- some, Yes, she's loved by one and

6 6 6 6 6 7 8 8 9 9 9 8 8 8 7

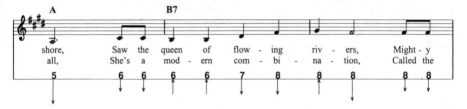

shore, Saw the queen of flow - ing riv - ers, Might - y
all, She's a mod - ern com - bi - na - tion, Called the

5 6 6 6 6 7 8 8 8 8 8

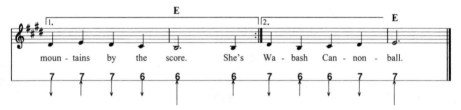

moun - tains by the score. She's Wa - bash Can - non - ball.

7 7 7 6 6 6 7 6 6 7 7

Chorus: Listen to the jingle,
The rumble and the roar,
Riding through the woodlands,
To the hills and by the shore.
Hear the mighty rush of the engine,
Hear the lonesome hobo squall,
Riding through the jungles
On the Wabash Cannonball.

Now, the eastern states are dandies,
So the western people say,
From New York to St. Louis
And Chicago by the way.
Through the hills of Minnesota
Where the rippling waters fall,
No chances can be taken
On the Wabash Cannonball. *Chorus*

Here's to Daddy Claxton,
May his name forever stand,
May he ever be remembered
Through parts of all our land.
When his earthly race is over
And the curtains 'round him fall,
We'll carry him to Glory
On the Wabash Cannonball. *Chorus*

Wildwood Flower

G Harmonica

I will twine and will min - gle my wav - ing black hair With the ros - es so

red and the lil - y so fair, The myr - tle so green of an

em - er - ald hue, The pale em - a - ni - ta and is - lip so blue.

Oh, he promised to love me, he promised to love
And to cherish me over all others above,
I woke from my dream and my idol was clay,
My passion for loving had vanished away.

Oh, he taught me to love him, he called me his flower,
A blossom to cheer him through life's weary hour,
But now he is gone and left me alone,
The wild flowers to weep and the wild birds to mourn.

I'll dance and I'll sing and my life shall be gay,
I'll charm every heart in the crowd I survey,
Though my heart now is breaking, he never shall know
How his name makes me tremble, my pale cheeks to glow.

I'll dance and I'll sing and my heart will be gay,
I'll banish this weeping, drive troubles away,
I'll live yet to see him regret this dark hour,
When he won and neglected his frail wildwood flower.

Worried Man Blues

G Harmonica

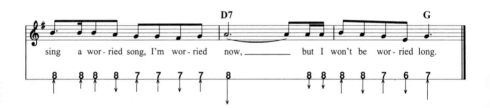

I went across the river and I lay down to sleep,
I went across the river and I lay down to sleep,
I went across the river and I lay down to sleep,
When I woke up - had shackles on my feet. *Chorus*

Twenty-nine links of chain around my leg,
Twenty-nine links of chain around my leg,
Twenty-nine links of chain around my leg,
And on each link, an initial of my name. *Chorus*

I asked the judge, "What's gonna be my fine?"
I asked the judge, "What's gonna be my fine?"
I asked the judge, "What's gonna be my fine?"
"Twenty-one years on the Rocky Mountain Line." *Chorus*

Twenty-one years to pay my awful crime,
Twenty-one years to pay my awful crime,
Twenty-one years to pay my awful crime,
Twenty-one years-but I got ninety-nine. *Chorus*

The train arrived, sixteen coaches long,
The train arrived, sixteen coaches long,
The train arrived, sixteen coaches long,
The girl I love is on that train and gone. *Chorus*

I looked down the track as far as I could see,
I looked down the track as far as I could see,
I looked down the track as far as I could see,
Litty bitty hand was waving after me. *Chorus*

If anyone should ask you, who composed this song,
If anyone should ask you, who composed this song,
If anyone should ask you, who composed this song,
Tell him it was I, and I sing it all day long. *Chorus*

The Wreck of the Old 97

A Harmonica

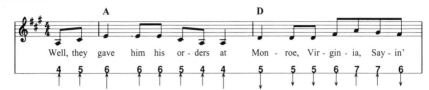

Well, they gave him his or - ders at Mon - roe, Vir - gin - ia, Say - in'

"Steve, you are way be - hind time, This is not 'thirty - ty- eight,' But it's

old 'nine - ty - sev - en,' You must put her in - to Dan - ville on time."

He turned and said to his black greasy fireman,
"Just shovel on a little more coal.
And when we cross the White Oak Mountain
You can watch old 'ninety-seven' roll."

He was going down the grade makin' ninety miles an hour,
When his whistle broke into a scream,
They found him in the wreck with his hand on the throttle,
He was scalded to death by the steam.

It's a mighty rough road from Lynchburg to Danville,
On a line on a three mile grade,
It was on this grade that he lost his average,
You can see what a jump he made.

Now ladies, take a warning from this awful story,
From this time now on learn,
Never speak harsh words to your true loving husband,
He may leave you and never return.

Ah, Poor Bird
Round

C Harmonica

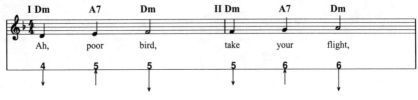

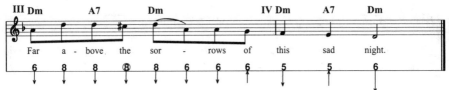

All the Pretty Little Horses

G Harmonica

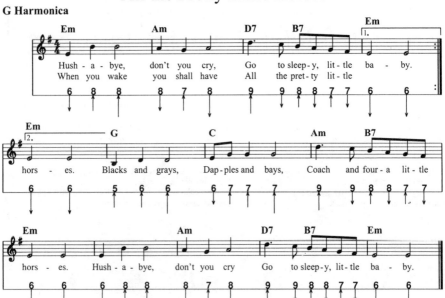

Hush-a-bye, don't you cry,
Go to sleepy, little baby.
Way down yonder in the meadow
Lies a poor little lambie.

The bees and the butterflies pecking out its eyes,
The poor little thing cried, "Mammy."
Hush-a-bye, don't you cry,
Go to sleepy, little baby.

Arkansas Traveler

D Harmonica

A traveler was riding by that day,
And stopped to hear him a-practicing away;
The cabin was afloat and his feet were wet,
But still the old man didn't seem to fret.
So the stranger said, "Now the way it seems to me,
You'd better mend your roof," said he,
But the old man said, as he played away,
"I couldn't mend it now, it's a rainy day."

The traveler replied: "That's all quite true,
But this, I think, is the thing for you to do;
Get busy on a day that is fair and bright,
Then patch the old roof till it's good and tight."
But the old man kept on a-playing at his reel,
And tapped the ground with his leathery heel:
"Get along," said he, "for you give me a pain;
My cabin never leaks when it doesn't rain."

A Tisket, A Tasket

D Harmonica

I dropped it, I dropped it,
Yes, on the way I dropped it,
A little girlie picked it up
And took it to the market.

A tisket, a tasket,
She took my yellow basket,
And if she doesn't bring it back,
I think that I will die.

Aunt Rhody

E Harmonica

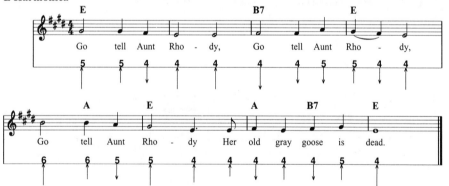

The one that she's been saving,
The one that she's been saving,
The one that she's been saving,
To make a feather bed.

She died in the millpond,
She died in the millpond,
She died in the millpond,
A-standing on her head.

The old gander's mourning,
The old gander's mourning,
The old gander's mourning,
Because his wife is dead.

The goslings are crying,
The goslings are crying,
The goslings are crying,
Because their mammy's dead.

Repeat first verse

Bill Groggin's Goat

G Harmonica

There was a man (there was a man), Now please take note (now please take

note), There was a man (there was a man) Who had a goat (who had a

goat). He loved that goat (he loved that goat), In - deed he did (in - deed he

did), He loved that goat (he loved that goat) just like `a kid (just like a kid)

One day the goat,
Felt frisk and fine;
Ate three red shirts,
Right off the line.
The man, he grabbed
Him by the back,
And tied him to
A railroad track.

Now, when that train
Hove into sight,
That goat grew pale,
And green with fright.
He heaved a sigh,
As if in pain;
Coughed up the shirts,
And flagged the train.

Billy Boy

C Harmonica

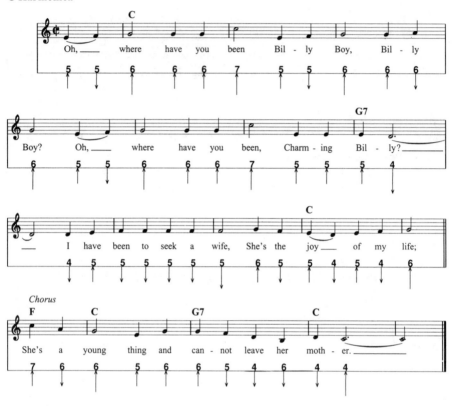

Oh, where have you been Bil - ly Boy, Bil - ly
Boy? Oh, where have you been, Charm - ing Bil - ly?
I have been to seek a wife, She's the joy of my life;
She's a young thing and can - not leave her moth - er.

Oh, where does she live,
 Billy Boy, Billy Boy?
Oh, where does she live,
 Charming Billy?
She lives on the hill,
Forty miles from the mill; *Chorus*

Did she bid you to come in,
 Billy Boy, Billy Boy?
Did she bid you to come in,
 Charming Billy?
Yes she bade me to come in,
And to kiss her on the chin; *Chorus*

And did she take your hat,
 Billy Boy, Billy Boy?
And did she take your hat,
 Charming Billy?
Oh yes, she took my hat,
And she threw it at the cat; *Chorus*

Did she set for you a chair,
 Billy Boy, Billy Boy?
Did she set for you a chair,
 Charming Billy?
Yes, she set for me a chair,
But the bottom wasn't there; *Chorus*

Can she bake a cherry pie,
 Billy Boy, Billy Boy?
Can she bake a cherry pie,
 Charming Billy?
She can bake a cherry pie,
Quick's a cat can wink her eye; *Chorus*

Can she make a feather bed,
 Billy Boy, Billy Boy?
Can she make a feather bed,
 Charming Billy?
She can make a feather bed,
That will rise above your head; *Chorus*

Boatman Dance

By Daniel Emmett

When the boatman gets on shore,
He spends his money and he works for more. *Chorus*

Never saw a pretty girl in my life,
But that she was a boatman's wife. *Chorus*

When the boatman blows his horn,
Look out, old man, your daughter is gone. *Chorus*

Sky-blue jacket and a tarpaulin hat,
Look out, boys, for the nine-tail cat. *Chorus*

E Harmonica

The Boll Weevil

The first time I seen the boll weevil,
He was sitting on the square.
The next time I seen the boll weevil,
He had all his family there,
Just a-looking for a home, just a-looking for a home. *2 times*

The farmer said to the weevil,
"What makes your face so red?"
The weevil said to the farmer,
"It's a wonder I ain't dead
Just a-looking for a home, just a-looking for a home." *2 times*

The farmer took the boll weevil,
And he put him in hot sand.
The weevil said, "This is mighty hot,
But I'll stand it like a man,
This'll be my home, this'll be my home." *2 times*

The farmer took the boll weevil,
And he put him in a lump of ice.
The weevil said to the farmer,
"This is mighty cool and nice,
It'll be my home, it'll be my home." *2 times*

The farmer took the boll weevil,
And he put him in the fire.
The boll weevil said to the farmer,
"This is just what I desire,
This'll be my home, this'll be my home." *2 times*

The boll weevil said to the farmer,
"You better leave me alone;
I ate up all your cotton,
And I'm starting on your corn,
I'll have a home, I'll have a home." *2 times*

The merchant got half the cotton,
The boll weevil got the rest.
Didn't leave the farmer's wife
But one old cotton dress,
And it's full of holes, and it's full of holes. *2 times*

The farmer said to the merchant,
"We're in an awful fix;
The boll weevil ate all the cotton up
And left us only sticks,
We got no home, we got no home." *2 times*

Buffalo Gals

C Harmonica

Oh, yes pretty boys, we're coming out tonight,
Coming out tonight, coming out tonight,
Oh, yes pretty boys, we're coming out tonight,
And dance by the light of the moon. *Chorus*

I danced with a gal with a hole in her stockin',
And her heel kept a-rockin' and her toe kept a-knockin',
I danced with a gal with a hole in her stockin',
And we danced by the light of the moon. *Chorus*

Clementine

E Harmonica

Chorus: Oh my darling, oh my darling, oh my darling Clementine,
You are lost and gone forever, dreadful sorry, Clementine.

Light she was, and like a fairy, and her shoes were number nine,
Herring boxes without topses, sandals were for Clementine. *Chorus*

Drove she ducklings to the water every morning just at nine,
Hit her foot against a splinter fell into the foaming brine. *Chorus*

Ruby lips above the water, blowing bubbles soft and fine,
Alas for me! I was no swimmer, so I lost my Clementine. *Chorus*

Deep Blue Sea

G Harmonica

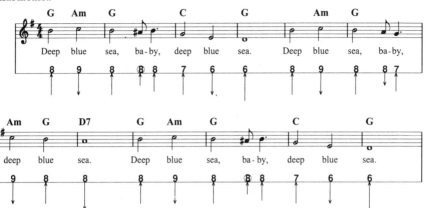

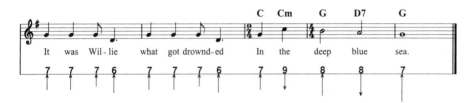

Dig his grave with a silver spade,
Dig his grave with a silver spade,
Dig his grave with a silver spade,
It was Willie what got drownded
In the deep blue sea.

Lower him down with a golden chain,
Lower him down with a golden chain,
Lower him down with a golden chain,
It was Willie what got drownded
In the deep blue sea.

Golden sun bring him back again
Golden sun bring him back again
Golden sun bring him back again
It was Willie what got drownded
In the deep blue sea. *Repeat first verse*

E - ri - e Canal

E Harmonica

We were loaded down with barly,
We were chock full up on rye,
And the captain he looked down at me
With his God damn' wicked eye. *Chorus*

The captain he came up on deck
With a spyglass in his hand.
And the fog it was so gosh-darn thick,
That he could not spy the land. *Chorus*

Two days out of Syracuse
Our vessel struck a shoal,
And we like to all been drownded
On a chunk o' Lackawanna coal. *Chorus*

Our cook she was a grand old gal,
She wore a ragged dress,
We hoisted her upon a pole
As a signal of distress. *Chorus*

The captain, he got married,
And the cook, she went to jail.
And I'm the only son of a gun
That's left to tell the tale. *Chorus*

Fillimiooriay

C Harmonica

In eight-een hun-dred and for-ty-one, I put my cor-du-roy

5 6 6 6 6 6 6 7 7 6 6 6 6 6 5

breech-es on, I put my cor-du-roy breech-es on, To work up-on the rail-way.

5 6 6 5 6 6 6 6 6 7 7 7 7 8 7 6 6

Chorus

Fil-i-mi-oo-ri-oo-ri-ay, Fil-i-mi-oo-ri-oo-ri-ay,

6 6 6 6 6 6 7 7 6 6 6 6 5 5 5 6

Fil-i-mi-oo-ri-oo-ri-ay, To work up-on the rail-way.

6 6 6 6 6 6 7 7 7 7 7 8 7 6 6

In eighteen hundred and forty-two,
I left the old world for the new,
Bad cess to the luck that brought me through.
To work upon the railway. *Chorus*

In eighteen hundred and forty-three,
'Twas then I met sweet Biddy McGee,
An elegant wife she's been to me,
While working on the railway. *Chorus*

In eighteen hundred and forty-four,
I worked again, and worked some more,
It's "Bend your backs," the boss did roar,
While working on the railway. *Chorus*

It's "Pat, do this," and "Pat, do that,"
Without a stocking or cravat,
And nothing but an old straw hat,
While working on the railway. *Chorus*

In eighteen hundred and forty-five,
They worked us worse than bees in a hive,
I didn't know if I was dead or alive,
While working on the railway. *Chorus*

In eighteen hundred and forty-six,
They pelted me with stones and sticks,
Oh, I was in a terrible fix,
While working on the railway. *Chorus*

In eighteen hundred and forty-seven;
Sweet Biddy McGee, she went to heaven,
If she left one child, she left eleven,
To work upon the railway. *Chorus*

Grey Goose

E Harmonica

My daddy went a-huntin',
Lord, Lord, Lord.
He was huntin' for the grey goose,
Lord, Lord, Lord.

And he went to the big wood,
Lord, Lord, Lord.
And he took along his shotgun,
Lord, Lord, Lord.

Along come a grey goose,
Lord, Lord, Lord.
Well, he up to his shoulder,
Lord, Lord, Lord.

And he rammed back the hammer,
Lord, Lord, Lord.
And he pulled on the trigger,
Lord, Lord, Lord.

And the shotgun went "boo-loo,"
Lord, Lord, Lord.
And the shotgun went "boo-loo,"
Lord, Lord, Lord.

Down he come a-fallin',
Lord, Lord, Lord.
He was six weeks a-fallin',
Lord, Lord, Lord.

And he put him on the wagon,
Lord, Lord, Lord.
And he took him to the white house,
Lord, Lord, Lord.

And your wife and my wife,
Lord, Lord, Lord.
They give a feather-pickin',
Lord, Lord, Lord.

They were six weeks a-pickin',
Lord, Lord, Lord.
They were six weeks a-pickin',
Lord, Lord, Lord.

And they put him on a par-boil,
Lord, Lord, Lord.
He was six weeks a-par-boil,
Lord, Lord, Lord.

And they put him on the table,
Lord, Lord, Lord.
And they put him on the table,
Lord, Lord, Lord.

And the fork couldn't stick him,
Lord, Lord, Lord.
And the knife couldn't prick him,
Lord, Lord, Lord.

Well, they throwed him in the hogpen,
Lord, Lord, Lord.
And the hogs couldn't eat him,
Lord, Lord, Lord.

Well, he broke the sow's jawbone,
Lord, Lord, Lord.
Well, he broke the sow's jawbone,
Lord, Lord, Lord.

So they took him to the sawmill,
Lord, Lord, Lord.
And he broke the saw's teeth out,
Lord, Lord, Lord.

And the last time I seen her,
Lord, Lord, Lord.
And the last time I seen her,
Lord, Lord, Lord.

She was flyin' 'cross the ocean,
Lord, Lord, Lord.
Had a long string of goslins',
Lord, Lord, Lord.

And they all went "Quonk, quonk,"
Lord, Lord, Lord.
And they all went, "Quonk, quonk,"
Lord, Lord, Lord.

Hey Ho, Nobody Home

G Harmonica

Round

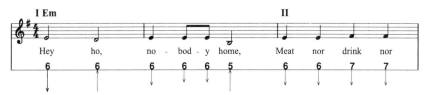

Hey Lolly, Lolly

D Harmonica

Married men will keep your secret,
  Hey lolly, lolly lo.
Single boys will talk about you,
  Hey lolly, lolly lo. *Chorus*

Two old maids a-sittin' in the sand,
  Hey lolly, lolly lo.
Each one wishin' that the other was a man.
  Hey lolly, lolly lo. *Chorus*

I have a girl, she's ten feet tall,
  Hey lolly, lolly lo.
Sleeps in the kitchen with her feet in the hall,
  Hey lolly, lolly lo. *Chorus*

Everybody sings the chorus,
  Hey lolly, lolly lo.
Either you're against us or you're for us,
  Hey lolly, lolly lo. *Chorus*

The purpose of this little song,
  Hey lolly, lolly lo.
Is to make up verses as you go along,
  Hey lolly, lolly lo. *Chorus*

I've Been Working on the Railroad

G Harmonica

Jennie Jenkins

E Harmonica

Will you wear green, oh, my dear, oh, my dear?
Will you wear green, Jennie Jenkins?
  No, I won't wear green,
    It's a shame to be seen. *Chorus*

Will you wear blue, oh, my dear, oh, my dear?
Will you wear blue, Jennie Jenkins?
  No, I won't wear blue,
    For the color's too true. *Chorus*

Will you wear yellow, oh, my dear, oh, my dear?
Will you wear yellow, Jennie Jenkins?
  No, I won't wear yellow,
    For I'd never get a fellow. *Chorus*

Will you wear brown, oh, my dear, oh, my dear?
Will you wear brown, Jennie Jenkins?
  No, I won't wear brown,
    For I'd never get around. *Chorus*

Will you wear beige, oh, my dear, oh, my dear?
Will you wear beige, Jennie Jenkins?
  No, I won't wear beige,
    For it shows my age. *Chorus*

Will you wear orange, oh, my dear, oh, my dear?
Will you wear orange, Jennie Jenkins?
  No, orange I won't wear,
    And it rhymes - so there! *Chorus*

What will you wear, oh, my dear, oh, my dear?
What will you wear, Jennie Jenkins?
  Oh, what do you care
    If I just go bare? *Chorus*

The Keeper

C Harmonica

The first doe he shot at he missed
The second doe he trimmed he kissed;
The third doe went where nobody wist
Among the leaves so green, O. *Chorus*

The fourth doe she did cross the plain;
The keeper fetched her back again;
Where she is now she may remain
Among the leaves so green, O. *Chorus*

The fifth doe she did cross the brook;
The keeper fetched her back with his crook;
Where she is now you must go and look
Among the leaves so green, O. *Chorus*

The sixth doe she ran over the plain;
But he with his hounds did turn her again,
And it's there he did hunt in a merry, merry vein
Among the leaves so green, O. *Chorus*

Kumbaya

C Harmonica

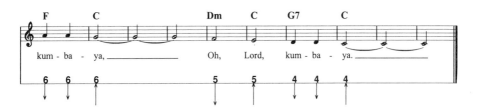

Someone's singing, Lord, kumbaya,
Someone's singing, Lord, kumbaya,
Someone's singing, Lord, kumbaya,
Oh, Lord, kumbaya.

Someone's dancing, Lord, kumbaya,
Someone's dancing, Lord, kumbaya,
Someone's dancing, Lord, kumbaya,
Oh, Lord, kumbaya.

Someone's weeping, Lord, kumbaya,
Someone's weeping, Lord, kumbaya,
Someone's weeping, Lord, kumbaya,
Oh, Lord, kumbaya.

Someone's shouting, Lord, kumbaya,
Someone's shouting, Lord, kumbaya,
Someone's shouting, Lord, kumbaya,
Oh, Lord, kumbaya.

Someone's praying, Lord, kumbaya,
Someone's praying, Lord, kumbaya,
Someone's praying, Lord, kumbaya,
Oh, Lord, kumbaya.

Michael, Row the Boat Ashore

D Harmonica

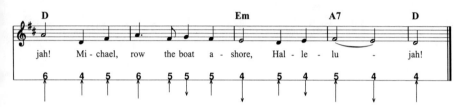

Sister, help to trim the sail,
  Hallelujah!
Sister, help to trim the sail,
  Hallelujah!

Michael's boat is a gospel boat,
  Hallelujah!
Michael's boat is a gospel boat,
  Hallelujah!

Jordan's River is chilly and cold,
  Hallelujah!
Chills the body but warms the soul,
  Hallelujah!

Jordan's River is deep and wide,
  Hallelujah!
Meet my mother on the other side,
  Hallelujah!

If you get there before I do,
  Hallelujah!
Tell my people I'm coming too,
  Hallelujah!

Repeat first verse

G Harmonica

Mrs. Murphy's Chowder

Won't you bring back, won't you bring back, Mrs. Murphy's chowder,
From each helping you'll be yelping for
a headache powder;
And if you dig in very far, you might
find a motor car,
In a plate of Mrs. Murphy's chowder. *Chorus*

Won't you bring back, won't you bring back, Mrs. Murphy's chowder,
You can pack it, you can stack it, all
around the larder.
The plumber died the other day; they
embalmed him right away,
In a bowl of Mrs. Murphy's chowder. *Chorus*

122

Oh, Sinner Man

C Harmonica

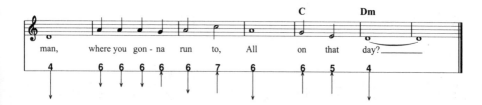

Run to the rock, the rock was a-melting,
Run to the rock, the rock was a-melting,
Run to the rock, the rock was a-melting,
  All on that day.

Run to the sea, the sea was a-boiling,
Run to the sea, the sea was a-boiling,
Run to the sea, the sea was a-boiling,
  All on that day.

Run to the moon, the moon was a-bleeding,
Run to the moon, the moon was a-bleeding,
Run to the moon, the moon was a-bleeding,
  All on that day.

Run to the Lord, oh, Lord, won't you hide me?
Run to the Lord, oh, Lord, won't you hide me?
Run to the Lord, oh, Lord, won't you hide me?
  All on that day.

Run to the Devil, the Devil was a-waiting,
Run to the Devil, the Devil was a-waiting,
Run to the Devil, the Devil was a-waiting,
  All on that day.

Oh, sinner man, you ought-a been a-praying,
Oh, sinner man, you ought-a been a-praying,
Oh, sinner man, you ought-a been a-praying,
  All on that day.

Oh, Susanna

C Harmonica

By Stephen Collins Foster

I come from Al - a - bam - a with a ban - jo on my
rained all night the day I left, The weath - er it was

knee. I'm _ goin' to Lou - 'si - an - a my Su - san - na for to
dry. The _ sun so hot I froze to death, Su - san - na don't you

Chorus

see. It _ cry. Oh, Su - san - na, oh, don't you cry for

me, For I come from Al - a - bam - a with a ban - jo on my knee.

I had a dream the other night
When everything was still.
I thought I saw Susanna
A-coming down the hill.

The buckwheat cake was in her month,
The tear was in her eye,
Says I, "I'm coming from the South,
Susanna, don't you cry." *Chorus*

Old Aunt Kate

C Harmonica

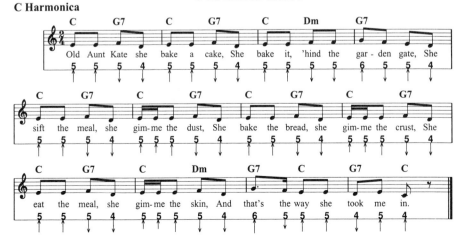

Old Aunt Kate she bake a cake, She bake it, 'hind the gar - den gate, She

sift the meal, she gim-me the dust, She bake the bread, she gim-me the crust, She

eat the meal, she gim-me the skin, And that's the way she took me in.

Oleanna

D Harmonica
Lyrics by Jerry Silverman

Music by Ditmar Meidel

Oh, my fel-low coun-try-men, If you'd be-come a mil-lion-aire, Just

head for O - le - an - na, All your fond - est dreams will come true there,

Chorus

O - le, O - le - an - na, O - le, O - le - an - na,

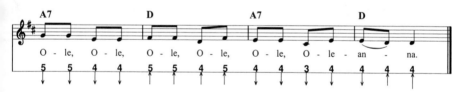

O - le, O - le, O - le, O - le, O - le, O - le - an - na.

Anywhere you take a walk,
And this is true, so I've been told,
If you chance to stub your toe,
'Twill be against a lump of gold. *Chorus*

Talk about good things to eat,
They've got them there, and that's no lie.
Apple strudle, apple dumplings,
Apple-sauce and apple pie. *Chorus*

When it's time to go to work,
And here you'll have a big surprise;
No sooner do you reach your job,
Than they close for holidays. *Chorus*

Oleanna, that's the place,
That's the place for you and me,
Where they pay you to relax,
And when you sleep, it's double fee. *Chorus*

Pay Me My Money Down

C Harmonica

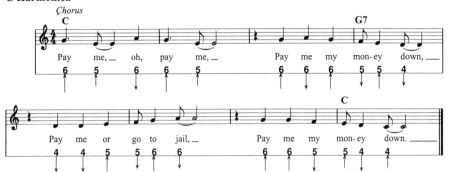

I thought I heard the captain say,
    Pay me my money down.
Tomorrow is our sailing day,
    Pay me my money down. *Chorus*

The very next day we cleared the bar,
    Pay me my money down.
He knocked me down with the end of a spar,
    Pay me my money down. *Chorus*

I wish I was Mister Howard's son,
    Pay me my money down.
Sit in the house and drink all the rum,
    Pay me my money down. *Chorus*

I wish I was Mister Steven's son,
    Pay me my money down.
Sit in the shade and watch all the work done,
    Pay me my money down. *Chorus*

There's lots more verses to this song,
    Pay me my money down,
But I guess we'd better be moving along,
    Pay me my money down. *Chorus*

Pick a Bale of Cotton

G Harmonica

Me and my gal can pick a bale of cotton,
Me and my gal can pick a bale a day. *Chorus*

Me and my wife can pick a bale of cotton,
Me and my wife can pick a bale a day. *Chorus*

Pop, Goes the Weasel

C Harmonica

All a-round the cob-bl-er's bench, The mon-key chased the wea-sel, The

mon-key thought 'twas all ___ in fun, Pop, goes the wea-sel!

I've no time to wait and sigh, No pa-tience to wait till by ___ and by, So

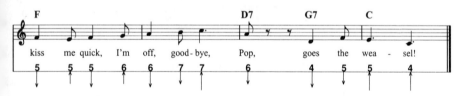

kiss me quick, I'm off, good-bye, Pop, goes the wea-sel!

A nickel for a spool of thread,
A penny for a needle,
That's the way the money goes,
Pop, goes the weasel!
You may try to sew and sew,
And never make something regal,
So roll it up and let it go,
Pop, goes the weasel!

I went hunting up in the woods,
It wasn't very legal.
The dog and I were caught with the goods,
Pop goes the weasel!
I said I didn't hunt or sport,
The warden looked at my beagle.
He said to tell it to the court,
Pop, goes the weasel!

My son and I we went to the fair,
And there were lots of people.
We spent a lot of money, I swear,
Pop, goes the weasel!
I got sick from all the sun,
My son, he got the measles,
But still we had a lot of fun,
Pop, goes the weasel!

This Old Man

D Harmonica

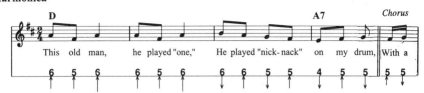

This old man, he played "two,"
He played "nick-nack" on my shoe. *Chorus*

This old man, he played "three,"
He played "nick-nack" on my tree. *Chorus*

This old man, he played "four,"
He played "nick-nack" on my door. *Chorus*

This old man, he played "five,"
He played "nick-nack" on my hive. *Chorus*

This old man, he played "six,"
He played "nick-nack" on my sticks. *Chorus*

This old man, he played "seven,"
He played "nick-nack" up in heaven. *Chorus*

This old man, he played "eight,"
He played "nick-nack" on my gate. *Chorus*

This old man, he played "nine,"
He played "nick-nack" on my spine. *Chorus*

This old man, he played "ten."
He played "nick-nack" once again. *Chorus*

Rolling home, rolling home,
Rolling, rolling, rolling home. *Chorus*

What Shall We Do With the Drunken Sailor

G Harmonica

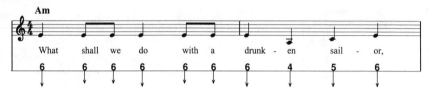

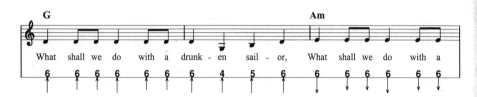

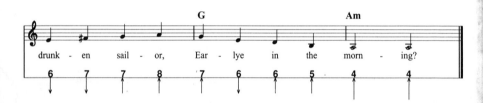

Chorus: Hooray, and up she rises,
Hooray, and up she rises,
Hooray, and up she rises,
Earlye in the morning.

Put him in a long boat till he's sober,
Put him in a long boat till he's sober,
Put him in a long boat till he's sober,
Earlye in the morning. *Chorus*

Hang him by the leg in a running bowline,
Hang him by the leg in a running bowline,
Hang him by the leg in a running bowline,
Earlye in the morning. *Chorus*

Put him in the scuppers with a hose pipe on him,
Put him in the scuppers with a hose pipe on him,
Put him in the scuppers with a hose pipe on him,
Earlye in the morning. *Chorus*

Shave his belly with a rusty razor,
Shave his belly with a rusty razor,
Shave his belly with a rusty razor,
Earlye in the morning. *Chorus*

That's what we'll do with the drunken sailor,
That's what we'll do with the drunken sailor,
That's what we'll do with the drunken sailor,
Earlye in the morning. *Chorus*